Genetic Bodybuilding:
Ectomorph, Endomorph, Mesomorph Training & Dieting Techniques

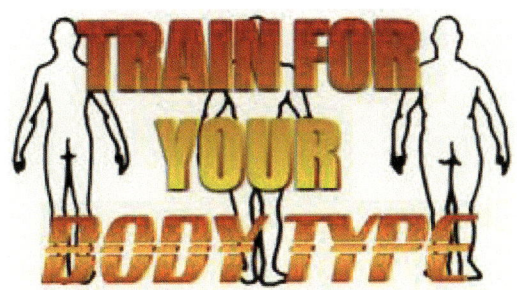

Genetic Bodybuilding: Ectomorph/Endomorph/Mesomorph Training & Dieting Techniques
By Tony Xhudo M.S., H.N., B.C.
Published by Dawn Xhudo
Copyright 2013 Dawn Xhudo

Muscle Growth Made Easy;
The Smart Way To Bodybuilding
For Your Genotype

Stop Wasting Valuable Time Training The Incorrect Way For Your Body-Type & Get The Results you Want!

Disclaimer:

The information contained in this book, including exercise programs, dieting, nutritional advice, and supplement usage or any other therapeutic programs are the result of experience and research by the author, and are presented here for educational purposes only. This information is only intended to provide helpful material on the subject addressed. Before you begin to attend to any health care, or exercise program, you should consult a health care professional regarding your specific situation.

All nutrients, diets, and supplements mentioned in this book are not to be taken without the advice of a medical doctor, naturopathic physician, registered dietician, and/or endocrine specialist. The author accepts no responsibility or liability for the misuse of any information or material contained in this book.

Dedication

We loved you yesterday
We love you still
We always have and
We Always will.

Pellumb
Fusha

Rest in peace my dear friend
You'll always live in my heart

-alex selimaj

This book is dedicated to my dear friend "Paulie Fusha" who believed in me and always managed to push me to train harder when I would seem to give up. A dedicated man to his family and friends, who will always be remembered for his pure heart and loyalty. The good Lord took you away, way too soon!

You will never be forgotten because you've touched my soul and embedded your smile in my thoughts, a smile that signifies belief in knowing what I can do! You've always came to me for advice on training, eager always to learn new things, and it is because of you that I write this book to share my knowledge to help those that need guidance in training. I love you, and even in heaven, I know your smiling down on me whenever I tend to slack off of my training, and that is why I continue to do what I love, even more so than before, because of you!

Rest In Peace My Dear Friend

Table of Contents

The Ultimate Guide To Genetic Bodybuilding;
Ectomorph/Endomorph/Mesomorph Training & Dieting Techniques

Are you doing everything possible to reach your genetic potential in building the muscle you so desire? <u>I doubt that many people actually do</u>, because they fail to realize or it is not mentioned to them that there are basically three body types that every human being falls under, and they are all following training and diet programs that their genetic make up does not allow them to reach their full genetic muscle building potential.

Virtually everyone is genetically different in regards to body development, and that is why I have put this book together, to help those individuals build the boy that they've always wanted. Genetics do ultimately determine our development and appearance, that is why it may be easier for some individuals to gain muscle much quickly than others, and for some of the others that do not have superior genetics, it is a bit more difficult.

But with the help of this book and the following information listed, I have listed some of the facts that should be considered according to which body type responds to what type of training regimen and diet to make the best amount of gains in the fast time possible. <u>Finally, now you can build the body that you have wanted and not fall short in following training routines and diets that were never really meant for your particular body type.</u>

You have to realize that what may work for one particular body type may not work for your metabolism, bone structure, height, and your given genetics, because they all come into play in the development of building muscle. Genetics will influence the rate of muscle gain and the eventual look gained from training and dieting. That is why for most mesomorphs it is relatively easy for them to gain muscle than the other two body types, ectomorphs and endomorphs. Each particular body type has their own set way of increasing muscular growth and with the help of this book you can actually reap the maximum benefit to your training and dieting techniques and reach your genetic potential.

Example, Arnold Schwarzenegger a mesomorph body type, looked more muscular after one year of training than most people do after 5 years of training. And research does show that some individuals respond better to strength training, while some barely respond, and some don't respond at all. Showing no results at all, creating the term "non-responders". But don't let that hold you back, because there are various factors that do come into play here. That is also why most of the muscle or bodybuilding books that advertise various training techniques always fail to point out that not all people of the various types of genetic body types will respond the same way.

This is so common today and that is also why so many people get so discouraged from training or take too long to produce good and satisfying results. Well, I'm going to clear that up for you and show you how you can make equally good gains as the superior body types that are out there, and with help of no steroids!

The bottom line is that for some lucky individuals that hit the genetic jackpot in building muscle, while others may have not, genetically speaking. But lucky for those individuals that may have fallen short of great genetics, there is strong scientific research that suggests that results that you may see in the gym are highly dependent on the efficacy of satellite cell-mediated myo-nuclear addition.

In other words, your muscles won't grow unless the satellite cells surrounding your muscle fibers donate their nuclei to your muscles so they can produce more genetic material to signal the cells to grow. We will take advantage of this concept and utilize what training method per geno-type will benefit you the most. It was also shown through trial and experimentation the difference between excellent responders in comparison to average and non-responders in strength training was due to satellite activation. Excellent responders have more satellite cells that surround their muscle fibers, as well as a remarkable ability to expand their satellite cell pool via training. This can be also achieved from those who lack the satellite cells through diet and training through gene expression.

This just shows that with the correct training techniques, and diet of course will help you increase your gene expression in response to training. Genetically, anything that negatively impacts the ability of the myofibers of muscle tissue to increase their number of myonuclei in response to training will reduce hypertrophy and strength potential. Nutrition and optimal training programing play a role in hypertrophy, and certain genotypes may be associated with hypertrophy regardless of inferior genetics.

It is a simple matter of tweaking your body type with the right kind of training, exercises, sets, reps, diet and supplement usage to figure out the best type of training program for your particular body type. Some body types respond best to a variety, some to volume, some intensity, frequency, and some to density. In this book we will explore to help you discover the best type of stimulus for your body type as you progress further along through the following chapters. Through my years of training and coaching the various body types of individuals, I have yet failed to come across any of the three basic body types that did not make the satisfactory gains that they have desired.

Results will come quickly for most that do put in the effort and dedication and follow whats best according to their body type. I can not lift the weights for you, but I can inform you of what works and what does not. So, if you have been a "Hard Gainer" and never really made the gains that you thought you would, you will be in for a surprise once you grasp the concept of training according to your particular body type and realize exactly what works for you and what doesn't. <u>Of course, the amount and rate of progress depends on your efforts, not your genetics that you may have thought was holding you back.</u>

And yes, genetics do make a difference, but smart training and the right diet and supplements can help you maximize what you thought your parents gave you in genetic material.

Good Luck to You, And Wishing You a Happy Journey On Your Way To Muscular Growth!..........Tony Xhudo, M.Sc./H.N./B.C.

INTRODUCTION

Smart Bodybuilding: Muscle Growth Made Easy
Phenotype Bodybuilding

This book or is for those who work out of building in the possible. Entailing simple procedures that will growth you can actually see 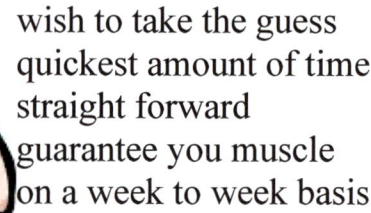 wish to take the guess quickest amount of time straight forward guarantee you muscle on a week to week basis.

The nutritional guidelines all proven to be muscle have been used by many those extra pounds muscle. laid out for you here are growth enhancers that who've desired to put on Whether to put on mass, bulk, and/or muscularity the results will definitely be worth your while. The supplements listed are many that you have read or heard about but did not realize how to utilize there full potential or what they can actually produce as far as results in growth are concerned.

Some of the supplements are *Glutamine, Citrulline, Vitamin D3, DHEA, Arginine, Leucine, DHEA, Flax Seed Oil, Fish Oil, Colostrum, Mucuna Prureins, Moomyimo, Cordyceps Extract, Bee Pollen, Royal Jelly, Deer Antler Extrac*t, Vit-D3, *Suma Root, Kre-Alkalin,* and many other effective ones that you may have thought to be bogus or sort of snake oil.

Dieting techniques will be touched on per body type. Foods like organic eggs, almond butter, cod liver oil, which provide natural hormonal health and natural "myostatin" inhibiting affect, spinach, for its high beta-ecdysterone use, cottage cheese for its high glutamine content, etc. And how you can use them to the best of your advantage.

Also, we will explore training techniques that respond best per individualized body types. You will get to see the best and proper exercises that effect the large major muscle groups which will help you produce the most amount of muscle growth possible in the shortest amount of time. This book is about helping you gain the maximum amount of muscle growth giving you straight information proven of what works and what doesn't work.

No more will you have to waist your time on exercise routines never really meant for your particular body type. When you eat, train, and employ the specific methods of body composition for your own body type and metabolism, you will respond to exercises in a much more efficient way.

The first part of this book you will learn the basics of muscle growth helping you to understand the science of muscle enhancement. And what you can do to speed things up. The second part will discuss the correct supplements to use and how best to apply them to your particular needs.

By using certain diet and nutritional protocols per specific body types and metabolisms, you will cut the time it takes to build muscle in half.

CHAPTER ONE

BASIC MUSCLE GROWTH 101: HYPERTROPHY & HYPERPLASIA

Every year more and there are more people, young, and old, looking for ways to enhance their self image and achieve a look of muscularity that will be admired from friends, and family. And why wouldn't you want to look muscular and strong anyways. Given the chance and simplicity, ask any teenager or man, would you like to have a physique that you can be proud of? They all will respond with an outstanding assurance of "Hell Yes!"

Well before we begin, its important for you to understand the basic concepts of how and why muscles grow to begin with. Knowing the physiology and bio-chemstry of muscle enhancement makes it a bit easier and kind of fun when working out. Now you will know why certain exercises do what they do to certain parts of the body, and also how certain exercises actually help to increase your hormonal out put towards muscle growth, like testosterone and growth hormone (GH).

Once all of this is basically understood you will begin to realize just how easy you can make any muscle group respond to any given exercise that you choose to do to improve what ever particular body part you wish to improve. Without getting to all the scientific jargon, we'll try to make this kind of easy for you to understand and apply towards your muscle development.

The science behind muscle building and growth is a complex biological process that involves certain biological steps. The good thing is that one really does not need to know everything about muscle hypertrophy and attain a Ph.D in the process, but all you really need to know is some basic steps that will help you build some serious muscle. You may have asked, so how do muscle's grow?

Well, let's find out in a more simplified way that will lead to a better understanding in allowing you to accomplish this. As your training in the gym with resistance exercise's, hypertrophy begins to take place. Muscle hypertrophy is an increase in the size of the muscle through an increase in the size of its component cells or fibers rather than an increased number of cells.

Hyperplasia is the splitting of muscle fibers that results in a greater number of muscle fibers the same size as the originals, or the growth of an organ due to to an increase in the number of cells. Hyperplasia occurs in response to ***heavy resistance exercise training***, with the emphasis being heavy resistance, key word here "resistance training".

Most theories are based on the idea that lifting weights or resistance training breaks down the muscle cells, and growth of the muscle results from the over-compensation in order to protect the body from future stress. Forcing the muscle to grow to adapt to the existing stressor at hand. Isn't that amazing! You see muscles have to grow because of the strain/resistance we put on them. Now when you apply the right diet and type of food and you do this on a continual basis with a scientific approach that you will begin to learn here, you will then realize, wow! I'm actually growing new muscle here!

Maximizing Your Muscle Fibers

The human body breaks down and rebuilds all of the muscles every 15 to 30 days, and rebuilding the muscle peaks 24 to 36 hours after training that can continue at an increased rate for as much as 72 hrs there after. Muscles also are composed of 2 basic type of fibers, *slow twitch and fast twitch muscle fibers.*

Muscle Structure

Aerobic exercise requires oxygen delivered via the blood vessels

Muscle fibres come in two types: fast twitch & slow twitch - they are mixed together

Slow twitch muscle fibers are those that are used in primarily endurance type of activities, such as long distance running, and weight resistance training with high repetitions of light weights will help to stimulate and develop these types of muscle fibers. Note that also training these types of muscle fibers (slow twitch) will not result in any gain of muscle mass. Just look at the world class long distance runners and see how lanky and thin these runners are.

Fast twitch muscle fibers are capable of a greater force that tire easily and have the least endurance than slow twitch muscle fibers. Fast twitch muscle fibers are those used in an explosive force as such activities like sprinting or power lifting. Weight resistance type of training with heavy weights will help to develop fast twitch fibers and potentially help you produce significant gains in muscle mass. Just think of the world class sprinters with those thick muscular legs.

So to build muscle and gain weight fast you must focus on the ___fast twitch muscle fibers___ during your training sessions and *emphasize* this important factor in your training regime. Regardless of genetics, given the proper *resistance training* and type of exercise and diet/supplements, your muscles have to adapt on grow!

This growth must take place to handle the load given by the demanding stress/resistance placed on it. Realize also, that many professional bodybuilders that were told that their genetics were not capable of producing a championship physique, because of narrowed shoulders, body type *(ectomorph, mesomorph, and endomorph)* were some of the past Mr. Olympia Champion bodybuilders, Larry Scott, being one of them.
He won the very first Mr. Olympia in 1965 and repeated again in 1966. We will touch on more of the 3 basic body types just listed to see where you may fall in one of them and how it pertains to your type of training protocols.

There are many studies that prove hyperplasia occurs in response to heavy resistance training. This has been proven many times, just look at say for example Olympic swimmers. The constant training on swimming repetitions on these swimmers you can see how long their muscle bellies lie, like on their bicep muscles, shoulders, long muscle lengths on the their thighs, and neck from the constant pulling movements as their about to do their stroke to propel themselves further along. Notice how all these swimmers have that tight sleek looking muscle development and abdominal muscles of steel as well.

This is the result of a form of resistance training done on water with the body's muscles responding to the demand placed on it. Also we can see this among sprinters and long distance runners. You can see how the two different types of muscle fibers come into play here with the sprinter muscles involving the fast-twitch muscle fibers. And the long distance runners involving the slow-twitch muscle fibers. So to build muscle and gain weight fast, you must focus on the fast-twitch muscle fibers during your training sessions and emphasize this important factor into your training routine keeping it in mind as you train month to month.

This means that <u>one must focus on training for strength and not endurance on any given workout day.</u> Training with heavy weights and low repetitions, and not with light weight and high repetitions. Also bare in mind that genetics do play an important part that determines the proportions of slow twitch muscle fibers to fast twitch muscle fibers that a person's muscle's contain. There are those individuals that contain a higher percentage of fast twitch fibers that will gain muscle mass relatively more than those with a high percentage of slow twitch muscle fibers, and they a called "Hard Gainer's". Through the techniques mentioned in this book you will learn how to acquire the muscle mass through hard and heavy compound movements that attack the large muscle groups of the body which in turn affect the smaller attached muscle parts.

Emphasize the training techniques designed for your specific goal and you will be on your way to achieving all the muscle growth you desire!

CHAPTER 2

Progressive Overload-Forcing Your Muscle's To Grow:

The determining factor in muscle growth is a progressive-overload of resistance training of muscle tissue. Muscle growth occurs only in a response to the stress put on the muscle. When an unusual over load *(stress)* is placed on the muscle tissue, a trauma occurs which causes small tears in the muscle fibers and the connective tissue of the muscle itself.

With a sufficient break in rest and a recovery period, the body will repair these small tears with a sound nutritional plan (*glutamine*) and additional protein intake, which will add size to the muscle fibers in order to better handle the over load that was placed on it previously. This is called "Hypertrophy".

Essentially what you are doing is stressing the muscle tissue, resting and recovering, feeding the muscle for repair; hence the growth process, and then repeating the stress level over again (***progressive-overload***) forcing the muscle to grow. This is the basic philosophy in a progressive weight training regimen designed for muscle building, a gradual increase in poundage of weights one lifts will create the need for the body to make the muscles stronger and bigger. Repetitions of 3 to 6 reps have been determined to be the ideal way to go. The increase in weight loads are determined by the body as a stress response, so the genetically programmed response will be to increase muscle mass in order for the muscle to better handle the additional load placed on it. ***So, know this, muscles will only grow when they are forced to grow! (a progressive-over load)***

Extra muscle growth will only occur providing you feed it correctly by giving yourself the required amount of nutrients and protein (post-workout recovery shake – hydrolysates).

We can not change our genetics, but we can increase our diet with a sound nutritional plan supplying the body with what it needs to put on and sustain new muscle mass through a resistance type of training we can change the demands we place on our muscles regardless of our genetic make up.

Through diet you can you can consistently provide the materials the body needs for additional growth of muscle to take place. The phenomenon known as the "pump" is partly a short lived example of an increased muscle cell volume, which is fluid (blood) moving into the cell of muscle tissue thereby causing it to stretch. It is this increase of cell volume that contributes to muscular growth. Research has also shown that supplements such as carbohydrates, lipids, and amino acids increases cellular movement and blood volume within the cell causing hypertrophy to take place thus an increase in muscle size.

The cells within the muscle tissue are involved in a process called ***"protein turn over rate"*** which is a balanced activity of breaking down the muscles and building it back up again.
Muscles are basically built up by mainly protein and water, and because of this you have to give your body a good amount of nutritional foods. Protein is the building blocks of what we are genetically made of, and the growth of skeletal muscle mass depends on protein turn over and cellular turn over. Protein synthesis is the way the body repairs and grows muscle tissue after exercise, and is the basic component of muscle.

The importance of protein intake can not be over stated and optimal protein intake based on many university studies state that it is the first step in creating an optimal environment inside your muscle cells where it can grow.

In this respect supplementing your diet with high quality protein shakes can be a big boost towards your muscular development. The human body synthesizes protein from diet at a rapid rate while the body is growing through adolescence and into adult hood. In an adult athlete, the synthesis of muscle protein is also related to how the muscles are being exercised. Muscular activity is a prerequisite of meaningful muscle development, built on protein synthesis.

During a physical workout, muscle will naturally break down, a process known as *"catabolism"*, this break down includes the physical separation of muscle fibers that comprise the muscle structure. The subsequent repair of the damaged muscle is known as *"anabolism"*, which is the build up and the growth of the existing and previously damaged muscle fibers. Protein synthesis is the mechanism by which the body affects this repair and muscle growth: as a very general proposition, when the body produces more synthesized protein than it consumes through its catabolic process, muscles then will be developed.

Protein is the nutrient that attracts most attention among athletes and gym enthusiasts. After all this is perfectly logical because protein is the "key" structural component of lean muscle tissue.

Overview:

When it comes to muscular growth, I would like to make a point clear. In the long run when training, if the desired outcome is gains in muscle mass, you have got to become stronger and productive during your workouts. So what ever workout your doing in building muscle mass, you have to challenge yourself in making your training sessions more challenging by employing the productive over-load principle discussed earlier.

Stick with compound exercises as stated earlier, these are the exercises that will get you to experience fast muscular growth, results that you can see in no time. Never workout the same muscle group or exercise when in heavy training for two days in a row, as this will result in stalemate and over training. Your rest periods should be no more than 60 seconds between sets. Stick with repetitions in 3 to 6 range for optimal growth and muscle mass.

Learn to also break up your exercises every 6 to 8 weeks as to avoid stalemate and boredom. Stick to and adhere to a sound nutritional diet plan providing your body with high quality protein from food sources and supplements. Understand that nutrition is more than half the battle in building muscle tissue and health. Get enough rest and sleep to recover from your heavy training sessions, and an occasional nap of 45 minutes to an hour, here or there would be of great benefit towards your muscle gains. This is when muscle growth and repair of damaged muscle cells occur.

Provide your body with ample amounts of protein every day keeping your body in a positive nitrogen state (anabolism) for muscle growth to occur and avoiding catabolism, the breakdown of muscle tissue.

Recognize the difference between fast and slow twitch muscle fibers as they correspond to muscle growth.

Note:

The following chapters will be much more explicit and more in depth on certain topics recently discussed, such as diet and protein requirements, sports supplementation, exercising, hormonal health for building muscle mass, over training, and the little secrets muscle magazines fail to touch on.

But that does not necessarily mean that those born with a high percentage of slow twitch fibers can not gain muscle mass just as easily as those born with fast twitch muscle fibers. Through a progressive weight lifting resistance course, any hard gainer can make expect to see the same results as those gifted good genetics, and **that is what this whole book is about**. We're going to make that happen for you!

Let's see now where your particular body type and bone structure falls under – Is it ***Ectomorph, Mesomorph, or Endomorph?*** Ok, we will break down each type for you to understand and how it pertains to you and your *training, diet, building your muscular growth* in the shortest amount of time possible and those results that I promised you! This way you can gain a better understanding of why in the past you did not make the gains you had wanted from following a particular training program you thought was going to work.

Endomorph   Mesomorph   Ectomorph

CHAPTER 3
BODY TYPES: Ectomorphs/Mesomorphs/Endomorphs
"How to Take Advantage of Your Genetic Potential To Build Muscle Fast"

Body types were introduced in the 1940's by Dr. William H. Sheldon, a noted great American Psychologist who devoted most of his life observing and classifying the wide spectrum of human bodies. While teaching at several universities and doing valuable research he came up with a system for classifying people into three basic body types. Dr. Sheldon's theory that described the 3 basic human body characteristics has now become an integral part of most literature that pertains to weight-loss, fitness and bodybuilding.

 If you are somewhere in between these three basic body types, this information will help you on how to train and respond based on your particular body type or

type
be
diet

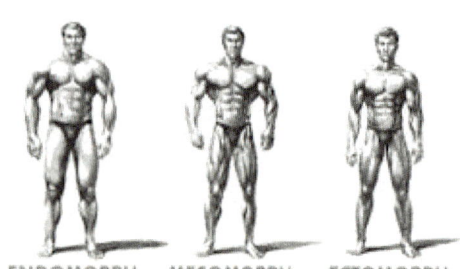

ENDOMORPH   MESOMORPH   ECTOMORPH

make

characteristics. Once you know what body you are, or possible combination of, you will better able to map out your plan of action on and training, and apply the correct type of exercises that you will respond to more efficiently for that particular body type to faster progress.

Bare   in mind also that its kind of impossible to change your body type, please do not think that if you change your plan to what worked for a mesomorph and your a ectomorph, its not going to happen and you will be in for a big disappointment wasting your efforts needlessly. Stick to your body type and apply what you've learned here and you will be on your way towards progress.

Endomorphs

Endomorphs gain weight by basically just looking at food. Their also known as the "fat" bodies of the group of body types. Their characterized by their body shape that is soft and round with usually short limbs as well as small hands and feet.

ENDORMOPH BODY BUILDER
JAY CUTLER

ENDOMORPH

In general, endomorphs have larger upper arms and thighs that appear soft, flabby, and out of shape in appearance, in comparison to their lower parts of their arms and legs. It is this type of appearance that makes endomorphs appear short and stocky. Endomorphs usually are jolly in nature and can build muscle fairly easily but will always fight the excess weight issue if they do not exercise or stay active. Their main basic features are:

- Soft body type un-athletic in appearance
- Flabby short upper arms with wide hips
- Underdeveloped muscles
- Round shape
- Over-developed digestive system

- Trouble losing weight
- Wide bone structure
- Slower metabolism
- Stores fat easily
- Generally gains weight easily
- And can generally gain muscle development easily as well.

The common strategy for gaining muscle mass written for ectomorphs or mesomorphs are not really optimal for the endomorph body type. This is due to their physiological and metabolic make up differences between these three phenotypes. Their metabolic rate is generally low which allows them to have a large number of fat cells and due to this, they could carry more fat than the average person. Their bones are large and thick with a large waist circumference that is generally large in proportion to their height.

While they due gain weight relatively fast and easily, endomorphs have the capacity to build muscle easily compared to the other body types, and without little effort. Bodybuilders that fit this description are Jay Cutler, 4 time Mr. Olympia winner. In order to stay fit and healthy and avoid gaining any extra weight, endomorphs need to be extremely strict with their diet and exercise routines. A healthy diet for endomorphs should be one that compromises low carbohydrates and low fat meals, together with regular exercising at least 3 to 5 times a week or some kind of weekly sports activity to stay in shape.

Weight Training For Endomorphs

<u>**Important Key Facts To Keep in Mind:**</u>

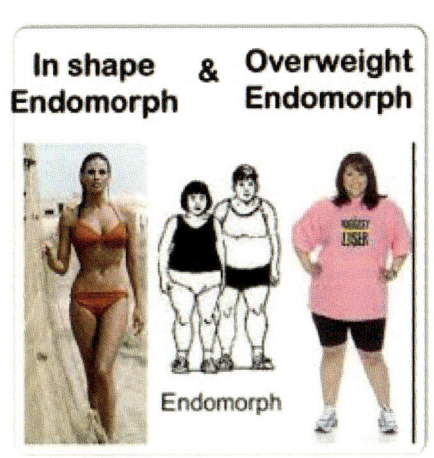

- *Endomorphs need more frequent workouts, especially aerobic conditioning*
- *Needs 2 to 3 exercises per body part*
- *Work on abdominals before workout routine*
- *Do whole body workouts for the first 6 to 8 weeks of the beginning of their program and then begin to do 4 day a week workouts.*
- *Training focus should entail to minimize body fat and speed up their metabolism, through diet, supplement usage, and exercises.*
- *Never stay on the same type of workouts, change exercises every now and then, alternate different set and rep schemes, super sets, and tri-sets should be incorporated.*
- *Change the training frequencies trying something different.*

- *Intensity levels should be high*
- *Sets for each body part should be high, 5 to 8 sets keeping your repetitions in the 9 to 12 range for the upper body and 12 to 25 for the lower body.*
- *Weight poundage should be mostly in the moderate range with occasional periods of heavy weight sessions for bulking up periods, (optional)*
- *Rest periods should be in between sets 60 seconds*
- *Endomorphs can utilize high intensity training principles such as burns, iso-tension, super-sets, tri-sets, descending sets, etc., to bring out maximum muscle shape and definition.*
- *Endomorphs can train more frequently, but do need 48 hours of rest before doing the same body workout for the same body part twice.*
- *Aerobic activity or cardio is a key component for endomorphs and can be included before workout as a warm up.*

Workout Routine For Endomoronphs

Because of their slow metabolism, endomorphs need to workout a bit more often than the other two somatypes. Four days of weight training split upper and lower body would be an ideal scenario for endomorphs.

This will ensure that the after burn of increased metabolic response form each training session will carry over into the following days. Over training is also a factor that they have to consider in being aware of. Cardio sessions should be included during their training sessions to jump start their metabolic rate.

Assuming the endomorph type is training for quality lean muscle growth based on their metabolic type, their main focus should be weight training. Because the increased amount of muscle mass they will gain, will increase their metabolic rate decreasing the chance of storing or holding any additional fat cells.

Endomorphs can employ several training strategies from high intensity to a low frequency type of training. They can start off with a 3 day whole body workout the first month and extend it to a 4 day a week training to a 5 or 6 day a week training sessions if they desire to bring it to a whole another level. Still over training could still be a possibility so keep that in mind when devising a workout routine once you've been accustomed to your training requirements.

Just as with the other body types, ectomorphs and mesomorphs. They should consider to start off with the heavy compound movements that affect the most major body groups of the body. Picking at least two exercises per body part. Then you can add isolation exercises to hone in the size and shape of the muscle-mass.

A sample 3 day a week whole body routine would look something like this:

3 Day a Week Whole Body Workout Routine

Mondays/Wednesday/Fridays: Start off with 15 to 20 minutes of Cardio

Legs – Heavy Full Squats - 2 x 12-10 reps; Leg Extension's – 2x 12-10
Chest – Barbell Bench Press – 2 x 12-10; Barbell pull overs – 2 x 12-10
Back – Heavy Barbell Rows or Cable Machine Rows - 2 x 12-10 ; Wide Grip Chins – 2 x12-10
Shoulders – Military press – 2 x12-10; Upright rowing – 2 x12-10
Biceps – Heavy Barbell Curls – 2 x12-10; Dumbbell Incline Curls 2 x 12-10; Barbell wirst curls or barbell reverse curls *(for fore arms-optional)*
Triceps – Close Grip Tricep press – 2 x12-10; Tricep Cable Press downs – 2x 12-10

Abdominals – Leg Raises 2 x (as many as you can do for 2 sets each)
Crunches 2 x (same as above)
Incline Sit-ups same as above.

Note: Your rest periods should be 60 seconds moving at a comfortable pace. Your workouts should not take you more than 1 hour. Keeping your intensity level upo at a good comfortable fast decent pace!

A sample 4 day split routine would look something like this:

- **Mondays Day 1 Chest/Shoulders/Triceps**
- **Tuesdays- Day 2 Legs/Back/Biceps**
- **Wednesday Day 3: Rest**
- **Thursday Day 4: Repeat Mondays Workout Routine**
- **Friday Day 5: Repeat Tuesdays Routine**
- **Saturday Day 6: Rest**
- **Sunday Day 7: Rest**

This is just an example for you to go by. In the later chapters I will include a guide of the compound movements that build the most muscle mass for you to pick and choose from along with some of the isolation exercises that you can include for shape and definition. You have to understand and realize that once you get comfortable with your workout routine, most people will often do exercises that they feel will benefit them the most or ones that they like to do, its matter of preference as one gets familiar with the various exercises that are out there.

But the key point here is to always include the large muscle building exercises (compound movements), high intensity that will recruit the maximum amount of muscle fibers like – *squats, dead-lifts, bench press, rowing, clean & jerk, high pulls, wide grip chins,* will also help to increase muscle building hormones in a positive way that will benefit your training. Try and plan your routine around these movements along with isolation exercises after the large muscle groups have been exhausted.

Always bare that in mind. I'm not going to say do this or do that exactly cause its impossible to know what one or all individuals like to do per body part. This is written to show and give one an example of the best beneficial exercise that will do the most good in the shortest amount of time.

Always take advantage of that anabolic window – post workout meals, this is the most opportune time "anabolic windows of opportunity" to put your body in this anabolic state. But, by not taking the advantage of this window of opportunity you will put your body in the opposite state "catabolism". Which is the state where your body is sacrificing muscle tissue instead of muscle growth. <u>Your goal is to try and stay in this anabolic mode as much as your body allows you to.</u>

Anabolic Windows:

<u>Phase 1</u> – comes 15 minutes following an intense workout and you have 45 minutes to an hour to capitalize. With a high protein meal.

<u>Growth Phase</u> – Takes place 1 to 2 hours following phase 1.

<u>Recovery Phase</u> – Takes affect following 2 hours after the growth phase.

<u>Your Secret Anabolic Window</u>? Is bedtime, a meal or protein shake, this is one of those crucial windows for most of your muscle growth to occur. By providing your body with the proper amount of high quality foods or protein shake (slow absorbing) necessary for optimal and continuous muscle growth.

<u>Keep a log</u> of everything you do during your workouts, exercises, sets, reps, record of weight used for each exercise, foods you eat, etc., progress made on supplement usage.

Pre-Workout/Post-Workout Ultimate Protein Shake Formulas

Pre-Workout Protein/Carb Shake

12 oz's of skim milk or water
15-25 grams of whey protein isolate's or hydrolyzed protein
30 to 45 grams of carb's (cyto carb by cyto sports)
10 grams of glutamine powder
5-10 BCAA's
5 grams of creating monohydrate
10 grams of colostrum (bonus) great for a natural igf-1 response
papaya enzyme or bromelian (helps with the digestion of proteins)

Post-Workout Protein/Carb/EFA's Shake
12 to 15 grams of skim milk
35 to 45 grams of whey protein hydrolysates
2 tablespoons of flax seed oil
5 grams of creating mono hydrate
10 grams glutamine
5-10 grams BCAA's

Bed Time Muscle Building Formula
12-15 oz's of skim milk
35 grams of micellar casein protein
10 grams of glutamine
10 grams of colostrum   (bonus additive) igf-1 response
papaya/bromelian enzymes

Note: This is the combination that I have been using myself and have been recommending to my clients that works very well, and the results are astonishing. On workout days I would consume 3 protein shakes a day along with my regular meals of breakfast, lunch, and dinner. On non-workout days I would consume my protein shakes 2 times a day being breakfast and bedtime, which is of the slow absorbing type of protein. You can also just stay on the 3 protein shakes a day Monday thru Friday, if you feel the need to put on the extra weight. These protein shake formula's that are listed are super charged with everything you need to maximize your growth potential.

Endomorph Diet Protocol

Because of the metabolic differences between the three phenotypes (ectomorph, endomorph, mesomorph) Endomorphs have the edge as far as gaining body weight and muscle. If an endomorph were to follow the same muscle building diet as an ectomorph they would definitely gain weight, but it would be mostly fat. Endomorphs need to find a dietary balance that will allow them to gain strength and lean muscle mass without adding body fat.

The emphasis here for endomorphs is gaining "Lean Muscle Mass" and that starts with introducing a diet that will help promote fat-free muscle mass. Gaining the extra body weight is not a problem for this particular body type, so we will have to be smart and include a diet that will produce the lean muscle mass choosing the correct type of foods as recommended below. By emphasizing a low-carb, high protein, and moderate fat diet plan you will ensure your gains to be lean muscle mass with minimal fat. Endomorphs typically tend to respond to carbohydrates adversely carbs.

So, aim your focus by simply reducing simply carbohydrate calories first, which means avoiding simply ordinary sugar found in most processed foods. Begin at first by assessing your current caloric expenditure (calories needed for normal body functions) and start reducing it, week by week.

Clean out your fridge and dump out all of the junk foods including the chips, dips, snacks, puddings, deserts, etc., as well as the high fatty processed foods. Change your eating habits and go to the supermarket and restock your fridge and cabinets with quality proteins, fats, and complex carbohydrates. Start by focusing on preparing yourself high quality meals and don't eat out as often from the popular fast food places advertised, McDonald's, Burger King, Taco Bell, etc.

When you need to snack on something breakout some vegetables, and high dense nutrient fruits or nuts. Once you get the hang of eating correctly, you will see how easy it can be to discipline yourself and probably won't go back to your old eating habits. Diet changes are absolutely one of the hardest adjustments to make among individuals that have been ruled for so long in eating junk foods that basically destroy your health little by little.

Summary of Attack: Lose Weight & Build Muscle By:

Starting to eat a clean diet
Figure out your caloric expenditure and reduce it week by week
Employ a low-carb, high protein, moderate diet
Restock your fridge with high quality protein foods & complex carbs
Stop eating at fast food restaurants
Eliminate all sugary by- products

High Performance Foods

Proteins:
Lean Meats, a variety of should include – *chicken breasts (boneless & skinless), turkey breasts, ground turkey meat fat-free, fresh fish -cod, tuna, salmon, haddock, halibut, tilapia, crabs, lobster, shrimp, egg whites or egg beaters, organic whole eggs, non-fat*

cottage cheese, lean sirloins, ground beef 90% fat free, roast beef is ok, cheese 2% reduced fat, milk 2%, skim milk, almond milk, soy milk, yogurts, buttermilk, other protein sources that are excellent – chlorella, spirulina, soy, almonds, pea nuts, peanut butter, baked beans, kidney, red, black, etc.

Protein Powders: purchase high quality protein powders that are of the **"hydrolyzed version"** of whey isolates that get absorbed within 15 minutes, these protein powders are very beneficial towards your muscle gains. They are a very high quality and can make the world of a difference in your development.

Protein powders come in several versions- **"fast absorbing"** for quick assimilation and digestion, and **"slow absorbing"** that digests rather slowly, sort of a time release way, 6 to 8 hours. And I do recommend that you utilize the two for both purposes.

Fast absorbing protein powders can be used one hour before training and immediately after training for the very important post-workout shake which is the critical "anabolic window" of opportunity!

Quality Recommended Brands of Fast Absorbing Protein Are: Proto-Whey by BioNutritional Research Group, Iso-100 by Dymatize Nutrition, Platinum Hydro Whey & Hydro-Builder by Optimum Nutrition, Iso-Fast by AllMax Nutrition, and VP2 by AST Sports Science. There are many other quality protein powders available, but to me these stand out the best by far according to their scientific make up and research that do get fast results!

Slow or Time-Release Protein Powders can be used during bedtime which is the most opportune time for muscle growth and recuperation. And can be used after breakfast keeping your body in a positive nitrogen state for 24 hour continuous feeding of amino acids!

Quality Recommended Brands of Slow Absorbing Protein Powders Are: Probolic-SR by MHP, 100% Casein Protein Powder by Optimum Nutrition, 100% Casein by Cyto Sports, Casein Protein Powder by 6 Star Pro Nutrition Elite Series, Micellar Matrix by ISS, and Pro-Complex by Optimum Nutrition.

Other Protein Blends contain a mixture of both fast and slow absorbing protein sources that nay have a blend consisting of 6 or 8 different sources of proteins. Which also include **MCT's,CLA's, and essential fatty acids along with vitamins and minerals**. You can add Flax Seed Oil to make it digest even slower and get the additional benefit of omega fatty acids as well.

Note: When preparing your foods trim away all the visible fat off of the meat and *poultry before cooking. **Broil, grill roast, poach, instead of frying** if possible and make it a habit of draining off fat that may occur while cooking.*

If choosing to fry your foods use olive oil, canola oil, safflower oil, and pea nut oil.

Vegetables:
Dark green leafy salads, asparagus, broccoli, cauliflower, green beans, spinach-natural steroidal saponins (high in beta-ecdysterone), mushrooms, kale, onions, garlic, all beans, avocados, brown rice, sweet potatoes, yams, baked potato, olives, tomatoes, basically all vegetables are great.

Grains:
wheat bread, rye, pumpernickel, granola, oat meal, cream of wheat, oat bran, barley, kashi medely, and stay away from white bread and white flower products.

Fruits:
Pineapples, apples, blue berries, straw berries, bananas, peaches, grapes, pears, papaya, raisins, watermelon, grape fruit, oranges, mango's, etc.

Obviously it would be wise to eliminate all junk foods, sweets, sugar products, cakes, cookies, ice cream, and fast food products while on your nutritional protocol. Once and awhile if temptation persists an occasional cheat of some ice cream or slice of cake I know is kind of hard to resist, but lets not make it a habit cause it can lead to over indulgence and then we're back where we started from, so learn a little discipline and if you do cheat spend the extra time working it off in the gym!

Important:

Endomorphs need to limit their carbohydrate intake as this is one of their physiological mechanisms that cause them to gain fat easily! The reason being is the over consumption of carbohydrates _leads to a large output of insulin_ thereby decreasing fat oxidation. Dietary carbs are necessary to gain muscle mass and for normal body functioning, and should not be totally eliminated from the diet. However, they should be consumed during when your body needs them, and most preferably should come from complex carbohydrate sources. This will satisfy your carbohydrate needs for energy and muscle glycogen.

It will benefit you most if you limit your carb intake to breakfast time and pre and post workout time. A sample breakfast menu can consist of *4 egg whites, 2 whole organic eggs, whole wheat bread with almond butter toasted, small serving of non-fat cottage cheese, oatmeal, and some straw berries and bananas.*

For your other meal a sample could be – Grilled salmon fillets, brown rice, green beans, dark grainy bread, and yams, with a glass of 2% milk.

 By consuming low Glycemic index carbs, brown rice, yams, etc., you can limit the insulin out put from the carbohydrate meal. Green vegetables and fruits are low in Glycemic carbs and do contain fiber and numerous nutrients that are very filling and satisfying. It is also very important to include the <u>essential fatty acids</u> in your diet and/or supplement their use with additional supplements that contain a <u>broad spectrum of these essential omega 3,6, and 9 fatty acids.</u> Essential fatty acid foods that you should be having are: *almonds, walnuts, Brazilian nuts, avocados, pea nuts and pea nut butter, flax oil, flax seeds ground, and olive oil.* These nutrients will help in the manufacture of your necessary hormones. I will include the ones that I feel are of great quality to your nutritional needs at the conclusion of this chapter.

Also Endomorphs should eat a little more on workout days isolating your carbs as recommended above on breakfast and lunch, and a little less on non-workout days. Adjust your carbs that you consume on non workout days according to the weight gain if you are gaining weight too fast!

Workout & Recovery Supplements

Proper Supplementation is Crucial Towards the Development of Fast Muscle Growth.

Glutamine – Probably one of the most over looked supplements for muscle growth has to be Glutamine. Hyped with anything that has to do with muscle enhancement and you will hear and read Glutamine being mentioned. The problem is that Glutamine gets so much notoriety in muscle magazines that most people fail to really grasp just how important Glutamine really is. I guess most people expect it to work really fast as if it were a steroid and they tend to give up on it, never really giving Glutamine a chance.

But I bet that if they knew that a lot of pro bodybuilders actually do use it but in large amounts they too then will give it a chance to prove that Glutamine does enhance muscle growth. You have have to realize that most of the muscle tissue is compromised of Glutamine more so than any other amino acid.

Glutamine prevents muscle catabolism, the tearing down of muscle, promotes muscle anabolism, which is basically muscle growth, enhances the immune system by converting into Glutathione the master anti-oxidant, and enhances muscle glycogen storage.
Glutamine's importance has gained new studies revealing its unique contribution to protein synthesis (muscle growth), anti-metabolic, and growth hormone enhancing

effects. Glutamine also plays a very important role in your body by aiding in recovery of the muscle cells from resistance training, a key factor towards muscular growth and enhancement.

The research in Glutamine is growing and its role in muscle development is only getting that much more interesting, but without getting into further detail and writing a book about Glutamine the most important thing that you need to know is that <u>2/3rds of the muscle cells are composed of Glutamine, the higher the Glutamine levels are in muscles – the faster the muscle grows. You must have adequate levels of glut amine in your body for continuous muscle growth to occur!</u> Glutamine also helps to build positive nitrogen atoms for nitrogen retention.

*Consume 5 to 10 grams of **<u>Glutamine</u>** 1 hour before workout routine and one protein shake of **<u>25 grams of "Hydrolyzed" protein powder</u>** for fast muscle uptake of important amino acids.*

<u>Good Brands of Glutamine to take are:</u>

<u>Glutamine-Sr</u> by MHP, *is a 12 hour patented feed delivery system.*
Important Information: 2/3rds of the muscle cells are composed of Glutamine, the higher the Glutamine levels are in muscles – the faster the muscle grows. You must have adequate levels of glut amine in your body for continuous muscle growth! Glutamine also helps to build positive nitrogen atoms for nitrogen retention.

<u>GL3 by AST Sports Science</u>, *a micronized version would be my second choice.*

<u>Recovery Supplement - "Glutathionine"</u> *- Considered the body's master anti-oxidant which plays a critical role in keeping the immune system functioning up to par and protecting cell strength and development, you would not want to be without Glutathionine. By keeping your Glutathionine levels high, you will be able to recover that much more quickly and have the extra endurance to succeed for the next days grueling workouts.*

Glutathionine is virtually found in every cell of the human body and by keeping levels of Glutathionine up you will help to speed up the muscle recovery process all the more efficiently which leads to muscle growth.

Raised Glutathionine levels helps increase strength and endurance. Those interested in physical fitness can benefit from a definite edge. (Journal of Applied Physiology 87: 1381-1385, 1999.)

<u>Creatine Monohydrate</u> – what would a weight lifting program be without mention of

creating Monohydrate, it works! And should always be included in every workout program from beginner to advanced.

<u>*Important Tip for older individuals (35 years and above) who are doing this program for muscle growth:*</u>

The amino acid Leucine: Extra grams of Leucine will help to boost the anabolic stimulus of proteins. By adding extra Leucine to your protein rich meals, older athletes will build up more muscle protein. When your still 30 years old and below your body will still react well to the anabolic stimulus of protein rich meals, as you get older your sensitivity to the stimulus declines.

A Leucine rich amino acid mix will strength the anabolic process in older athletes and help to support the catabolic process (break down of protein). Leucine supplements are gaining much popularity in the supplement field among strength and power athletes that are over 35 years old looking for that extra help in their anabolic process of muscle growth. <u>Adding at least 5 to 10 grams of Leucine before your large protein meals of the day, adding two times a day of extra Leucine on workout days will be most beneficial.</u>

<u>Leucine Supplements are available and note worthy brands are, Source Naturals, AllMax Nutrition, Twin Labs, Now, and Jarrow Nutrition.</u>

<u>*Most Needed Supplements For Nutritional Workouts*</u>

The mainstay supplements that should be in every one's workout nutritional protocol should be the two different protein sources fast & slow utilized for different requirements thus creating a positive nitrogen balance priming your anabolic growth potential.

- "Hydrolyzed" protein powders from the recommended brands listed for each phenotype.
- The "Slow" digesting protein powders recommended.
- The amino acid "Glutamine" taken on a daily basis. See brands recommended earlier.
- The branch chain amino acid "Leucine" or "BCCA's"

These supplements are basically standard do help immensely in the growth of muscle tissue and aid in the recovery period. Other necessary supplements that help to increase growth hormone, testosterone, and insulin potentiators are also mentioned in later chapters in this book that you can pick and choose from as needed to further fuel your growth.

(Sources – AM Journal of Physiology Endocrinol Metab. 2006 Auhust; 291(2):E381-7)

Abstract: A higher portion of Leucine is required for optimal stimulation of the rate of muscle tissue protein synthesis by essential amino acids in the elderly; Christos S. Katsanos, Hisamine Kobayashi; Metabolism Unit, Shriners Burns Hospital, Galveston, Texas; Febuary 17 2006.

Antonio J. Gropper Street C. Glutamine: a potentially useful supplement for athletes. Can J. Appl Physiology. 1999; 24:1-14.

ECTOMORPHS:

Fragile, small bone structure
Flat Chested
Delicate build
Young Appearance
Tall and thin
Lightly muscled
Stoop and narrow shoulders
Large brain
Has trouble gaining weight
Muscle growth takes longer
Fast metabolism

ECTOMORPH

ECTOMORPH BODY BUILDER
FRANK ZANE

Ectomorphs are basically skinny, thin, tall, small bone structure types that have thin bones and small muscles. Their limbs are relatively long in proportion to the torso and their shoulders often droop and appear narrow.

Ectomorphs are not naturally strong because of their corresponding small bone structure and small muscles. They also tend to be fragile in shape, posting a lean physique, flat chested and have to basically work hard to gain muscle mass. They seem to struggle gaining weight no matter how much they eat, despite the possibility of having a high and unhealthy body fat percentage. This could be due to the fact that they have a fast metabolism as well.

A typical Ectomorph will appear tall and thin with a slight muscle definition. On women, this body type will bode well, but not men that are trying to gain muscular body weight. Their main focus should be to work hard and efficient choosing the corrective type of exercises that will do the most good according to their bone stand metabolism.

Weight training should be done fairly heavy and their workout pace should be slower with longer rest periods between sets.

Their diet plan should be strict eating with the most nutrient dense type of foods, emphasis on quality, and not junk foods either. Feeding times should be often, more than they are use to with the calories being high in number.

Aerobic activities, like sports, dancing, jogging, or high caloric expenditure type of activity should definitely be kept to a minimum until you are basically where you want to be with weight and looks.

Know that body types respond to differently to both training and nutrition. As a result of this, it's vital that you apply and become aware of what body type you have so that you can maximize and design an effective workout/nutritional program that corresponds best to your needs.

Ectomorph Workout Routine

Know that as an Ectomorph you can achieve the dream physique with a little hard work and dedication. The only disadvantage, is the one that you place on yourself in not believing that it can be accomplished.
In general an Ectomorphs workout should involve overall less training sessions and volume. Because your workout recovery capacity is just not up to par with the recovery capabilities as an Endomorph or a mesomorphs.

Your focus should be by adding more intensity to your training program than volume and adequate rest periods between sets. Hard work, efficiency, and intensity are the key requirements for Ectomorphs to build the muscle mass they long for.

Key Facts to be aware of are:

Super-fast metabolism that burns calories fast and efficiently.

Keep your activity levels to a minimum. Cardio not really recommended but if so for cardiovascular health, do minimum amount, 15 minutes or so.

Diet, Training, and Rest periods are very important. Workout sessions should never be more than 60 minutes, with 45 minutes being optimum.

Strength Training should be a progressive resistance type on a weekly basis, even if it's at a minimum of 2.5 pound increase in weight. Remember, muscle fibers will grow to adapt to the increased workload.

Intensity, hard work, efficient workouts, are the key to maximize training efforts, and not volume of exercises and high sets of 6 to 8 or more of an hour or two hour training sessions that should be avoided. **When past the advanced level of training then additional sets can be added.**

Use basic heavy basic power movements that hit the deep muscle fibers.

Keep repetitions in the 10 to 5 range.

Use 1 to 2 body parts each workout to large target muscle groups.

Train each body part once a week.

Change exercise routines at least every 2 months.

Watch out for over training, (it can slow down your muscle progress)

NOTE: *If gains in muscle and strength remain slow, shock your body into new growth with techniques as 10 sets of 10 reps for one exercise "only" per body part, and only do this shocking technique every 2 months. Or add other techniques such as super-sets, tri-sets, giant sets, and burns, but do not rely on staying on it for too long during your workout program.*

Weight-lifting training will be a push/pull routine done with heavy compound movements and minimal isolation exercises per muscle group which will be added after 6 weeks of training. Because of the super-fast metabolism type weight training will also burn calories, so it is recommended to do a 3 day a week workout routine, example – Mon/Wed/Fri or Tues/Thurs/Saturday with 2 day rest period at the end of the week.

An optional shock technique will be added which includes super-sets. The heavy compound movements should be based on a pyramid scheme per each particular body part. Keep your rest periods between 2-3 minutes between each set. Abs are optional if you want to include them at the end of your workouts. Always have a supply of water with you drinking in between sets, its always very important to keep your muscles well hydrated even if your not thirsty. Believe it or not it will help with the growth of new muscle fibers.

Important Tips For Muscle Growth; An Excellent Diet and Proper Supplementation are Crucial Towards the Development of Fast Muscle Growth.

Consume 5 to 10 grams of **Glutamine** 1 hour before workout routine and one protein shake of **25 grams of "Hydrolyzed" protein powder** for fast muscle uptake of important amino acids.

Good brands of Protein powder & Glutamine to take are: The fast absorbing "whey hydrolysates" protein powders are the ones to use before and after training. 15 to 25 grams are required to prime your body and fuel muscle growth before your workout. Remember, you are what your able to absorb!

Glutamine-Sr by MHP, is a 12 hour patented feed delivery system. Important Information: 2/3rds of the muscle cells are composed of glutamine, the higher the Glutamine levels are in muscles – the faster the muscle grows. You must have adequate levels of glut amine in your body for continuous muscle growth! Glutamine also helps to build positive nitrogen atoms for nitrogen retention

Iso-Fast "100% Hydrolyzed" Protein by Dymatize Nutrition

VP2 Whey Isolates by AST Sports Science.

Iso-Flex by AllMax Nutrition – 90% pure bio-active protein (what the pro's use) great science behind it.

Pro-Whey by BioNutritional Research Group: This is another 100% Pure Hydrolyzed protein powder, containing 100% Micro-peptide formula (Incredible results!)

These specific protein powders are the ones that I feel are the top choice "fast absorbing" protein powders if you want fast results the price!

Recovery Supplement - "Glutathionine" - Considered the body's master anti-oxidant which plays a critical role in keeping the immune system functioning up to par and protecting cell strength and development, you would not want to be without Glutathionine. By keeping your Glutathionine levels high, you will be able to recover that much more quickly and have the extra endurance to succeed for the next days grueling workouts.

Glutathionine is virtually found in every cell of the human body and by keeping levels of Glutathionine up you will help to speed up the muscle recovery process all the more efficiently which leads to muscle growth.

Raised glutathionine levels helps increase strength and endurance. Those interested in physical fitness can benefit from a definite edge. (Journal of Applied Physiology 87: 1381-1385, 1999.)

<u>Creatine Monohydrate</u> *– what would a weight lifting program be without mention of creating Monohydrate, it works! And should always be included in every workout program from beginner to advanced.*

<u>Important Tip for older individuals (35 years and above) who are doing this program for muscle growth:</u>

The amino acid Leucine: Extra grams of Leucine will help to boost the anabolic stimulus of proteins. By adding extra Leucine to your protein rich meals, older athletes will build up more muscle protein. When your still 30 years old and below your body will still react well to the anabolic stimulus of protein rich meals, as you get older your sensitivity to the stimulus declines.

A Leucine rich amino acid mix will strength the anabolic process in older athletes and help to support the Catabolic process (break down of protein). Leucine supplements are gaining much popularity in the supplement field among strength and power athletes that are over 35 years old looking for that extra help in their anabolic process of muscle growth. <u>Adding at least 5 to 10 grams of Leucine before your large protein meals of the day, adding two times a day of extra Leucine on workout days will be most beneficial.</u>

(Sources – AM Journal of Physiology Endocrinol Metab. 2006 Auhust; 291(2):E381-7)

Abstract: A higher portion of leucine is required for optimal stimulation of the rate of muscle tissue protein synthesis by essential amino acids in the elderly; Christos S. Katsanos, Hisamine Kobayashi; Metabolism Unit, Shriners Burns Hospital, Galveston, Texas; Febuary 17 2006.

**Workout Routine
"Push-Pull"**

Workouts are done 3 days a week doing one body part per week for the first 6 to 8 weeks. Once a week pick and choose two exercises that you wish to super-set: Example Bench press and Rowing exercises, to shock the muscles and prevent boredom/stale mate, muscles will eventually become accustomed to the routine at hand, so at times it is necessary to throw in super-sets to wake them up!

<u>Day 1 – Chest & Back:</u>

Barbell Bench press – (warm up set should be a medium to light for 12 to 20 reps)

- 1st set 12 reps.
- 2nd set 10 reps.
- 3rd set 8 reps
- 4th set 6 reps

Barbell Rowing or Cable Rowing:

- 1st set 12 reps
- 2nd set 10 reps
- 3rd set 8 reps.
- 4th sct 6 rcps

Weighted Bar Dips: (1st set done with no weights, second, third, and fourth set adjust the weight using the belt with the chain attached to it to perform the required amount of reps. Do full movements going all the way down with chin placed on chest, and go all the way up. Do full concentrated movements, no cheating or sloppy movements.)

- 10-12 reps. **(increase the weight with each descending set)**
- 10-8 reps
- 8-6 reps
- 6-4 reps

Wide Grip Lat Pull Downs: 12, 10, 8, 6 reps. (increase the weight with each descending set)

Deadlifts: 10, 8, 6, 4 (increase the weight with each descending set)
Last exercise is your abdominal muscles, (optional) if you choose to do so!

Leg raises (reps are as many as you can do per movement)
Crunches
Sit-ups

NOTE: All three of these movements are done in one continuous tri-set, one after another with no brake in between, except when you are done with all three movements, start off with 2-3 tri-sets and increase as you go along in your workout program.

Day 2 – Legs & Biceps:

Barbell Full Squats: make sure you have assistants when performing this exercise, a spotter to help control the weight and balance. Or you can perform it on a Smith-Machine which actually acts as a spotter allowing better control on the up and down movement.

- 12, 10, 8, 6 reps

Pull-Overs: 12, 10, 8, 8 (done with a comfortable weight allowing you to perform full and strict movements. (this exercise is a good one to super-set with the squats allowing you to help increase and expand your chest muscles and size!

Barbell Curls: 12, 10, 8, 6 reps, Use a shoulder width grip on this movement. By spacing the width of your grip it will effect different aspects of your bicep development. You can vary your grip to achieve the full effect of this particular movement.

Leg Presses – 12, 10, 8, 6 reps (increase weight as you pyramid down)

Barbell or Dumbbell Preacher Curls: 12, 10, 8, 6 reps. (same as above)

Abs; optional

Day 3 – Shoulders/Traps/Triceps:

Military Press: 12, 10, 8, 6 reps (pyramid same as above) (can be done on Squat rack or Smith machine)

Upright Rowing – 12, 10, 8, 6 reps (start off with the first reps of 12 with shoulder width grip and the second set of 10 reps the same, then space your hand grip thumbs apart on the 3rd set of 8 and 4th set of 6 reps)

Clean & Jerk: 10, 8, 6, 4 reps (this is a great over all body mass developer, make sure your wearing a weight lifting belt for this particular exercise)

Note: For those of you that have never performed this movement, start off with a comfortable weight that you can handle fairly easily, in a spacious uncrowded area lean over with hands spaced shoulder width and grab the bar, now in one controlled movement pull the bar up to the chest line area in one continuous sweep as if you were going to press the bar overhead but your not actually going to press it over your head, but just holding it at chest level, then you begin to lower it back down again to the floor. Repeat this procedure for several required reps as stated above.

Close Grip Tricep Press: 12, 10, 8, 6 reps (pyramid down increasing the weight) Place hand grip about thumbs apart as if you were performing a bench press.

Close Grip Tricep Press Downs on Cable Machine: 12, 10, 8, 6 reps

Abs: optional

Very Important: At the end of your workout you need to take advantage of the anabolic window of opportunity now, this is very important step for fast muscular growth. Always make it a habit in consuming <u>30 to 45 grams of a fast source of a "Hydrolyzed" Protein powder shake</u>, with <u>two table spoons of Flax seed oil</u>, and <u>one scoop of creating monohydrate immediately</u> after your workouts!

Always take advantage of that anabolic window – post workout meals, and unfortunately there are only a few of these anabolic windows of opportunity to put your body in this anabolic state. But by not taking the advantage of this window of opportunity you will put your body in the opposite state "catabolism". Which is the state where your body is sacrificing muscle tissue instead of muscle growth. Your goal is to try and stay in this anabolic mode as much as your body allows you to.

Anabolic Windows:

Phase 1 – comes 15 minutes following an intense workout and you have 45 minutes to an hour to capitalize. With a high protein meal.

Growth Phase – Takes place 1 to 2 hours following phase 1.

Recovery Phase – Takes affect following 2 hours after the growth phase.

Your Secret Anabolic Window? Is bedtime meal or protein shake, this is one of those crucial windows for most of your muscle growth to occur. By providing your body with the proper amount of high quality food necessary for optimal muscle growth. (see chapter on diet).

Keep a log of everything you do during your workouts, exercises, sets, reps, record of weight used for each exercise, foods you eat, etc.

Pre-Workout/Post-Workout Ultimate Protein Shake Formula's

Pre-Workout Protein/Carb Shake

12 to 15 oz's of skim milk or water
15-20 grams of whey protein isolate's or hydrolyzed
30 to 45 grams of carb's
10 grams of glutamine powder
5-10 bcaa's
5 grams of creating monohydrate
10 grams of colostrum (bonus) great for a natural igf-1 response
papaya enzyme or bromelian

Post-Workout Protein/Carb/EFA's Shake
12 to 15 grams of skim milk
35 to 45 grams of whey protein hydrolysates
2 tablespoons of flax seed oil
5 grams of creating mono hydrate
10 grams glutamine
5-10 grams bcaa's

Bed Time Muscle Building Formula
12-15 ozs of skim milk
35 grams of micellar casein protein
10 grams of glutamine
papaya/bromelian enzymes
10 grams of colostrum   (bonus additive) igf-1 response

Note: This is the combination that I have been using myself and have been recommending to my clients that works very well, and the results are astonishing. On workout days I would consume 3 protein shakes a day along with my regular meals of breakfast, lunch, and dinner. On non-workout days I would consume my protein shakes 2 times a day being breakfast and bedtime. You can also just stay on the 3 protein shakes a day Monday thru Friday, skipping the weekends to give your digestive system a break. These protein shake formula's that are listed are super charged with everything you need to maximize your growth potential.

Important: Once you get familiar with the exercises and routine you can add additional exercises to change it up or change the frequencies of your workout days. Example being – you can do a 2 day on and 1 day off for 4 workouts a week, like Mon/Tues, Wed-Off, Thurs/Fri and Sat/Sun – Off.

Or you can do whole body workouts 3 days a week doing a complete upper and lower body routine in a day. Try and see in what your body will respond best to as you go along and experiment with the various workout routines that are available.

Remember that every one is different, and everyone responds differently to what works best for them, this normally takes time to figure out as you try different things and routines. It took me years of training to know that my particular body type made the fast gains when I focused on one body part per week allowing me to recuperate and grow that more faster, if I wanted extra size that is.

That is basically how it works for mostly everyone, being accustomed to what works best for you! Trial and error is what at stake here!

Food & Diet For Ectomorph's

With the training out of the way diet is going to be 75% of your wanted gains in muscularity to put quality mass, and trust me you will! If you follow things out accordingly. The one thing about Ectomorph is that they basically can eat what ever they want, including junk foods more so than any other body types, because of their fast metabolism and not really put on any body fat.

But still, Ectomorphs will need to stick with high quality protein sources and healthy essential fatty acids as much as possible in order to try and reset their metabolism with the help of certain foods and supplements. Its important for Ectomorph types to eat at least every three hours with each meal consisting of quality protein, of 1.5 grams per pound of body weight, and essential fats with some complex carbs thrown in the mix for sustained energy levels. A guide of good food sources are listed below as an example:

Quality Protein Sources:

Lean Steaks, 95% lean ground beef, Chicken breasts, Turkey, Tuna, Egg whites, whole eggs are OK, Beans, Whey Proteins, Salmon, Spirulina, Chlorella, Soy, Milk, Skim Milk, Cottage cheese (high in Glutamine),

Vegetables & Grains:

Brown rice, whole wheat products, broccoli, asparagus, Green beans, Spinach (excellent source of iron & Beta-Ecdysterones), Sweet potatoes, peanut butter, pea nuts, all nuts are great source of proteins & essential fatty acids, Olives, Olive oil, Canaola Oil, Pea nut Oil, avocados, Oatmeal, dark grain breads.

Fruits: All fruits are great, supplies the body with important vitamins, minerals, and live enzymes.

Dietary Essential Fats: Are very important for proper body functioning and hormone production. Most people have an unhealthy balance of these fatty acids.

Good sources are – almonds, walnuts, almond butter, peanut butter and pea nuts, avocados, flax seeds, olive oil, eggs, fish, sardines, salmon, tuna, mackeral. And omega 3 fish oil supplements, Krill oil. Look for quality name brand sources like Carlson's, Udo's Choice, Source Naturals when purchasing your fatty acid supplements. Trust me brand names do make a difference in quality ingredients.

Ectomorph body types simply have to eat a lot to grow! There's no way around that. That is the primary factor that governs your growth potential, calories! You need to take in more calories than you burn, if you eat less than you burn you will then lose weight! You don't need to force feed yourself either, just try and introduce more feeding times day by day and soon you will adapt to the extra feeding times, and besides as your muscles start to grow from the supplements, workouts, and diet, you will actually begin to notice that your hunger level will increase on a natural basis. So, stick with that concept in mind on a daily level and just watch your muscles g-r-o-w! Providing of course your following your workout routine. You will thank yourself later on, as your muscles begin to grow on a week to week basis!

I don't really wish to choose and make this kind of difficult or lengthy in regard to reading on the explanation, but just trying to give you an idea of basic idea's on what you can do to gain muscle fast. The core understanding of using the correct weight training exercises, diet, and supplements, and of how to combine the whole thing to the best of your advantage.

Most Needed Supplements For Nutritional Workouts

The mainstay supplements that should be in every one's workout nutritional protocol should be the two different protein sources fast & slow utilized for different requirements thus creating a positive nitrogen balance priming your anabolic growth potential.

- "Hydrolyzed" protein powders from the recommended brands listed for each phenotype.
- The "Slow" digesting protein powders recommended.
- The amino acid "Glutamine" taken on a daily basis. See brands recommended earlier.
- The branch chain amino acid "Leucine" or "BCCA's"

These supplements are basically standard do help immensely in the growth of muscle tissue and aid in the recovery period. Other necessary supplements that help to increase growth hormone, testosterone, and insulin potentiators are also mentioned in later chapters in this book that you can pick and choose from as needed to further fuel your growth.

MESOMORPHS

Mesomorphs are characterized by a muscular frame with relatively low amounts of body fat. They also have the ability to gain weight/muscle and can lose fat weight when a given plan of a healthy, low fat, high protein type of diet is followed. These body types are the ones that are envied the most, and if you fall into this body, you are in luck!

MESOMORPH

MESOMORPH BODY BULDER
ARNOLD SHWARZENEGGER

They have the ability to build a quality physique of a master piece status. When optimally conditioned, mesomorphs can gain lean muscle-mass quickly and don't actually lose it quickly either. However, they also have the tendency to gain fat and may sometimes have trouble losing fat.

Most athletes are generally mesomorphs and this could be due to their ability to build strong muscles and bones. The female mesomorphs have a typical hour glass shape, while the males generally have a rectangle shape. Their bones are strong and thick, which allows them to build amounts of muscle that they can carry on their large frame. These types of body's are also ideal for bodybuilding as they posses both the strength and physical ability to gain muscle mass that ranks championship status.

They have the more desirable body among the other two body types falling right in the middle of the spectrum. Once the desirable body composition is achieved, the mesomorph can usually just maintain, making sure to continue exercising regularly and living a healthy lifestyle.

The mesomorph characteristics and typical traits are:

- Large head, broad shoulders, and narrow waist (wedge-shaped).
- Muscular body, with a strong forearms and thighs
- Very little body fat
- Genetically gifted; greatest bodybuilding potential.
- Long torso, full chest, good shoulder to waist ratio.
- Hourglass shaped for women
- Gains or Loses weight easily

Training For Mesomorphs, Workout Diet & Supplements

Key Facts To Keep In Mind:

- Mesomorphs respond well to heavy basic movements along with shaping exercises.
- Variety being the key to muscle growth, changing exercise routines often.
- Alternate with high intensity and low frequency training programs to prevent boredom and burnout.
- Keep reps in the 8 to 12 range for most of the body parts, except for lower body should be 20 to 25 rep range.
- Sets could as high as 6 to 8 per body part.
- Because of the genetic advantage, be careful for over training and the notion of more equals better gains, a big mistake!
- Mesomorphs need to constantly keep the body off guard with varying the training intensity with exercises, sets, weight increases, and reps
- Be sure to include isolation exercises along with basic heavy compound movements.
- Range of motion should always be a steady full motion of up and down movements not sacrificing form for weight.
- Do at least 3 cardio workouts per week for at least 20 to 30 minutes.
- Get 8 to 9 hours of sleep
- Never train a body part that has not fully recovered from previous workouts.
- Keep protein intake to at least 1.5 gram per pound of body weight.
- Keep carbohydrate intake moderately high, about 60% of total calorie intake; choosing vegetables, brown rice, low fat beans, lentils, and pasta and whole grains.
- Limit fat intake; try and stay lean with a diet containing 15 to 20% total fats, essential fats.
- Eat a variety of lean protein foods such as chicken breasts, turkey, egg whites, lean beef, and fresh fish.
- Drink at least 2.5 liters (80 ounces) of water daily, hydration is very important for muscle growth and recovery, helps keep the body functioning more efficiently with the elimination of toxins from excess sweating during workouts.

For bodybuilding, a mesomorph body type is the best body type of the three to be in. most of the mesomorph body types have a muscular frame from either playing sports when in high school or the college years. Their genetics are their greatest strong point for bodybuilding and competition of bodybuilding. They simply grow muscles fairly easily as if they were a chia pet needing water. Their bodies are actually designed for bodybuilding and the stress of lifting weights.

They can handle high intensity training sessions fairly well because they have excellent recovery capabilities. Their bodies are physically stronger and therefore less prone to injury. And because of this they can handle advanced training programs very well. For Mesomorphs it will be pointless to really include a set type of workout schedule for them because basically they will thrive on what ever exercises they actually decide to do, so I will just list the important compound movements and some isolation exercises just to give you an idea of some of the important ones that I feel that have stood out and produced some of the best body parts we have seen by most of the professional bodybuilders.

Mesomorphs just have to decide what kind of workout is best suited for them. For example here is a list of programs that you can employ that will benefit you the most:

- High frequency training
- German volume training
- Vince Gironda's 8x8 training routine
- Reg Park's 5x5 heavy training routine
- Mike Mentzer's Heavy Duty "HIT" Program
- 3x3 training program
- Bulgarian Training program

Workout training principles that you can do are:

- Super-sets
- Tri-sets
- Giant sets
- Burns
- Forced reps
- Negatives
- Rest-pause training
- Compound sets
- Staggered sets
- Pre-Exhaustion training

Pre-Workout/Post-Workout Ultimate Protein Shake Formulas

Pre-Workout Protein/Carb Shake

12 to 15 oz's of skim milk or water

15-20 grams of whey protein isolate's or hydrolyzed whey isolates
30 to 45 grams of carb's
5 grams of glutamine powder
5 bcaa's
5 grams of creating monohydrate

Post-Workout Protein/Carb/EFA's Shake
12 to 15 oz's of skim milk
35 to 45 grams of whey protein hydrolysates
2 tablespoons of flax seed oil
5 grams of creating mono hydrate
5-10 grams glutamine
5-10 grams bcaa's
5-10 grams of colostrum (bonus) great for a natural igf-1 response
papaya enzyme or bromelian

Bed Time Muscle Building Formula
12-15 oz's of skim milk
35 grams of micellar casein protein
5-10 grams of glutamine
papaya/bromelian enzymes
10 grams of colostrum   (bonus additive) igf-1 response

Note: This is the combination that I have been using myself and have been recommending to my clients that works very well, and the results are astonishing. On workout days I would consume 3 protein shakes a day along with my regular meals of breakfast, lunch, and dinner. On non-workout days I would consume my protein shakes 2 times a day being breakfast and bedtime. You can also just stay on the 3 protein shakes a day Monday thru Friday, skipping the weekends to give your digestive system a break. These protein shake formula's that are listed are super charged with everything you need to maximize your growth potential.

Sample Workout Program For Mesomorphs

To start off your workout program, my recommendation to get you going to see results fast would be a 3 day a week workout routine working each body part one time for the week to get the muscle growth primed laying the foundation for future muscle-mass enhancement. Heavy compound movements obviously would be the right choice here. Plus one isolation exercise per body part.

Monday Day: Legs, Chest, and Abs.

Legs:
Full Squats – 2-3 sets x 12-8 reps (warm up set 20 reps)
Leg Extensions – 2-3 sets x 12-8
Calf raises – 2-3 sets x12-15

Chest
Barbell bench press – 2-3 sets x 12-8 reps
Barbell pull overs – 2-3 sets x 12-8
Dumbell incline Press – 2-3 sets x 12-8
Weighted Dips – 2-3 sets x 12-8

ABS: are optional but if you choose to do so!
Sit ups 3 sets x (till fatigued) till you get your set rhythm down.
Leg raises - same as above
Crunches – same as above

Wednesday: Shoulders/ Triceps/Biceps/ABS

Military Barbell press – 3-4 sets x 12-8
Upright rowing (varying the grip from thumbs apart to shoulder width) 3-4 sets x 12-8
Side dumbbell lateral raises – 3-4 sets x 12-8
Heavy dumbbell shrugs – 3-4 sets x 12-8

Triceps:
Close grip tricep barbell press 3-4 sets x 12-8
Close grip tricep press downs cable machine – 3-4 sets x 12-8
Dumbbell One arm extensions – 3-4 sets x 12-8

ABS: Same as above

Fridays: Back/Biceps/Abs

Back:
Barbell end rowing 3-4 sets x 12-8
Wide Grip pull downs 3-4 sets x 12-8
Dead lifts – 3-4 sets x 12-8
Heavy Barbell shrugs – 3-4 sets x 12-8
High Pulls – 3-4 sets x 8-6

Biceps:
Heavy barbell curls – 3-4 sets x 12-8
Dumbbell alternate curls – 3-4 sets x 12-8

Barbell preacher bench curls – 3-4 sets x 12-8
Barbell wrist curls – 3-4 sets x 12-8

Note: Mesomorphs should keep their workout time to 1 hour or less, keeping the intensity up with 60 seconds of rest periods between sets. Even though mesomorph have the capability to train an hour plus, it would still be a good idea to keep within reason, to avoid over training. Thought to keep in mind is – train with a progress work load attitude on a weekly basis, this will ensure you are making gains on a positive note.

Very Important: At the end of your workout you need to take advantage of the anabolic window of opportunity now, this is very important step for fast muscular growth. Always make it a habit in consuming 30 to 45 grams of a fast source of a "Hydrolyzed" Protein powder shake, with two table spoons of Flax seed oil, and one scoop of creating monohydrate immediately after your workouts!

Always take advantage of that anabolic window – post workout meals, and unfortunately there are only a few of these anabolic windows of opportunity to put your body in this anabolic state. But by not taking the advantage of this window of opportunity you will put your body in the opposite state "catabolism". Which is the state where your body is sacrificing muscle tissue instead of muscle growth. Your goal is to try and stay in this anabolic mode as much as your body allows you to.

Anabolic Windows:

Phase 1 – comes 15 minutes following an intense workout and you have 45 minutes to an hour to capitalize. With a high protein meal.

Growth Phase – Takes place 1 to 2 hours following phase 1.

Recovery Phase – Takes affect following 2 hours after the growth phase.

Your Secret Anabolic Window- Is bedtime meal or protein shake, this is one of those crucial windows for most of your muscle growth to occur. By providing your body with the proper amount of high quality food necessary for optimal muscle growth. (see chapter on diet).

Keep a log of everything you do during your workouts, exercises, sets, reps, record of weight used for each exercise, foods you eat, etc.

Diet For Mesomorph Training

The primary factor that determines whether you gain or lose weight/muscle is your caloric intake (how many calories you eat). If you eat more calories than you burn (hypercaloric) you will gain weight/muscle and if you burn more calories than you eat (hypocaloric) you will lose weight/muscle. When you eat exactly the same amount of calories as you burn it is called a maintenance caloric diet.

Mesomorphs trying to gain lean muscle growth need to eat a hypercaloric diet consisting of a ration of 55% protein, 35% carbs, and 10% fats, or 50% protein, 35% carbs, 15% fats, or however which way works best for you as you go along in your training regimen. You can also determine maintenance caloric intake by taking your body weight and multiply it by 15; this gives you your total calories to be consumed each day. For mesomorphs trying to gain muscle, it is recommended to take in an extra 250-500 calories above their maintenance calorie intake. I keep my protein intake slightly higher than my carbohydrate intake, and my essential fatty acid intake between 10-15%, especially during training.

A good idea when consuming carbohydrates is to limit their use when you need it most to aid muscle growth and limit fat gains, making breakfast time and pre/post workout time as the two best possible choices. Carbohydrates should come from complex sources, see list below.

High Performance Foods For Mesomorphs

Proteins:
Lean Meats, a variety of should include – *chicken breasts (boneless & skinless), turkey breasts, ground turkey meat fat-free, fresh fish -cod, tuna, salmon, haddock, halibut, tilapia, crabs, lobster, shrimp, egg whites or egg beaters, organic whole eggs, non-fat cottage cheese, lean sirloins, ground beef 90% fat free, roast beef is okay, cheese 2% reduced fat, milk 2%, skim milk, almond milk, soy milk, yogurts, buttermilk, other protein sources that are excellent – chlorella, spirulina, soy, almonds, pea nuts, peanut butter, baked beans, kidney, red, black, etc.*

Note: When preparing your foods trim away all the visible fat off of the meat and poultry before cooking. Broil, grill roast, poach, instead of frying if possible and make it a habit of draining off fat that may occur while cooking.

If choosing to fry your foods use olive oil, canola oil, safflower oil, and pea nut oil.

Vegetables:
Dark green leafy salads, asparagus, broccoli, cauliflower, green beans, spinach-natural steroidal saponins (high in beta-ecdysterone), mushrooms, kale, onions, garlic, all beans, avocados, brown rice, sweet potatoes, yams, baked potato, olives, tomatoes, basically all vegetables are great.

Grains:
wheat bread, rye, pumpernickel, granola, oat meal, cream of wheat, oat bran, barley, kashi medely, and stay away from white bread and white flower products.

Fruits:
Pineapples, apples, blue berries, straw berries, bananas, peaches, grapes, pears, papaya, raisins, watermelon, grape fruit, oranges, mango's, etc.

Obviously it would be wise to eliminate all junk foods, sweets, sugar products, cakes, cookies, ice cream, and fast food products while on your nutritional protocol. Once and awhile if temptation persists an occasional cheat of some ice cream or slice of cake I know is kind of hard to resist, but lets not make it a habit cause it can lead to over indulgence and then we're back where we started from, so learn a little discipline and if you do cheat spend the extra time working it off in the gym!

Important:
Mesomorphs need to limit their carbohydrate intake as this is one of their physiological mechanisms that cause them to gain fat easily! The reason being is the over consumption of carbohydrates leads to a large output of insulin thereby decreasing fat oxidation. Dietary carbs are necessary to gain muscle mass and for normal body functioning, and should not be totally eliminated from the diet. However, they should be consumed during when your body needs them, and most preferably should come from complex carbohydrate sources. This will satisfy your carbohydrate needs for energy and muscle glycogen.

It will benefit you most if you limit your carb intake to breakfast time and pre and post workout time. A sample breakfast menu can consist of *4 egg whites, 2 whole organic eggs, whole wheat bread with almond butter toasted, small serving of non-fat cottage cheese, oatmeal, and some straw berries and bananas.*

For your other meal a sample could be – Grilled salmon fillets, brown rice, green beans, dark grainy bread, and yams, with a glass of 2% milk.

 By consuming low glycemic index carbs, brown rice, yams, etc., you can limit the insulin out put from the carbohydrate meal. Green vegetables and fruits are low in glycemic carbs and do contain fiber and numerous nutrients that are very filling and satisfying. It is also very important to include the essential fatty acids in your diet and/or supplement their use with additional supplements that contain a broad spectrum of these essential omega 3,6, and 9 fatty acids. Essential fatty acid foods that you should be having are: almonds, walnuts, Brazilian nuts, avocados, pea nuts and pea nut butter, flax oil, flax seeds ground, and olive oil. These nutrients will help in the manufacture of your necessary hormones. I will include the ones that I feel are of great quality to your nutritional needs at the conclusion of this chapter.

Also endomorphs should eat a little more on workout days isolating your carbs as recommended above on breakfast and lunch, and a little less on non-workout days. Adjust your carbs that you consume on non workout days according to the weight gain if you are gaining weight too fast!

Dietary Essential Fats: Are very important for proper body functioning and hormone production. Most people have an unhealthy balance of these fatty acids.

Good sources are – almonds, walnuts, almond butter, peanut butter and pea nuts, avocados, flax seeds, olive oil, eggs, fish, sardines, salmon, tuna, mackeral. And omega 3 fish oil supplements, Krill oil. Look for quality name brand sources like Carlson's, Udo's Choice, Source Naturals when purchasing your fatty acid supplements. Trust me brand names do make a difference in quality ingredients.

I don't really wish to choose and make this kind of difficult or lengthy in regard to reading on the explanation, but just trying to give you an idea of basic idea's on what you can do to gain muscle fast. The core understanding of using the correct weight training exercises, diet, and supplements, and of how to combine the whole thing to the best of your advantage.

Supplement Protocol

Important Tips For muscle Growth; An Excellent Diet and Proper Supplementation are Crucial Towards the Development of Fast Muscle Growth.

Consume 5 to 10 grams of **Glutamine** *1 hour before workout routine and one protein shake of* **25 grams of "Hydrolyzed" protein powder** *for fast muscle uptake of important amino acids.*

Good brands of Protein powder & Glutamine to take are: The fast absorbing "whey hydrolysates" protein powders are the ones to use before and after training. 15 to 25 grams are required to prime your body and fuel muscle growth before your workout. Remember, you are what your able to absorb!

Glutamine-Sr by MHP, *is a 12 hour patented feed delivery system.*
Important Information: 2/3rds of the muscle cells are composed of glutamine, the higher the glutamine levels are in muscles – the faster the muscle grows. You must have adequate levels of glut amine in your body for continuous muscle growth! Glutamine

also helps to build positive nitrogen atoms for nitrogen retention

<u>Iso-Fast "100% Hydrolyzed" Protein</u> by Dymatize Nutrition

<u>VP2 Whey Isolates</u> by AST Sports Science.

<u>Iso-Flex</u> by AllMax Nutrition *– 90% pure bio-active protein (what the pro's use) great science behind it.*

<u>Pro-Whey</u> by BioNutritional Research Group: *This is another 100% Pure Hydrolyzed protein powder, containing 100% Micro-peptide formula (Incredible results!)*

These specific protein powders are the ones that I feel are the top choice "fast absorbing" protein powders if you want fast results the price!
The Importance of Glutamine

<u>Proper Supplementation is Crucial Towards the Development of Fast Muscle Growth.</u>

Glutamine – Probably one of the most over looked supplements for muscle growth has to be Glutamine. Hyped with anything that has to do with muscle enhancement and you will hear and read glutamine being mentioned. The problem is that glutamine gets so much notoriety in muscle magazines that most people fail to really grasp just how important glutamine really is. I guess most people expect it to work really fast as if it were a steroid and they tend to give up on it, never really giving glutamine a chance.

But I bet that if they knew that a lot of pro bodybuilders actually do use it but in large amounts they too then will give it a chance to prove that glutamine does enhance muscle growth. You have have to realize that most of the muscle tissue is compromised of glutamine more so than any other amino acid.

Glutamine prevents muscle catabolism, the tearing down of muscle, promotes muscle anabolism, which is basically muscle growth, enhances the immune system by converting into glutathione the master anti-oxidant, and enhances muscle glycogen storage.

Glutamine's importance has gained new studies revealing its unique contribution to protein synthesis (muscle growth), anti-metabolic, and growth hormone enhancing effects. Glutamine also plays a very important role in your body by aiding in recovery of the muscle cells from resistance training, a key factor towards muscular growth and enhancement.

The research in glutamine is growing and its role in muscle development is only getting that much more interesting, but without getting into further detail and writing a book about glutamine the most important thing that you need to know is that 2/3rds of the muscle cells are composed of glutamine, the higher the glutamine levels are in muscles – the faster the muscle grows. You must have adequate levels of glut amine in your body for continuous muscle growth to occur! Glutamine also helps to build positive nitrogen atoms for nitrogen retention.

Consume 5 to 10 grams of **Glutamine** 1 hour before workout routine and one protein shake of **25 grams of "Hydrolyzed" protein powder** for fast muscle uptake of important amino acids.

Good Brands of Glutamine to take are:

Glutamine-Sr by MHP, is a 12 hour patented feed delivery system.
Important Information: 2/3rds of the muscle cells are composed of glutamine, the higher the glutamine levels are in muscles – the faster the muscle grows. You must have adequate levels of glut amine in your body for continuous muscle growth! Glutamine also helps to build positive nitrogen atoms for nitrogen retention.
GL3 by AST Sports Science, a micronized version would be my second choice.
Important Tip for older individuals (35 years and above) who are doing this program for muscle growth:

Recovery Supplement - "Glutathionine" - Considered the body's master anti-oxidant which plays a critical role in keeping the immune system functioning up to par and protecting cell strength and development, you would not want to be without Glutathionine. By keeping your Glutathionine levels high, you will be able to recover that much more quickly and have the extra endurance to succeed for the next days grueling workouts.

Glutathionine is virtually found in every cell of the human body and by keeping levels of glutathionine up you will help to speed up the muscle recovery process all the more efficiently which leads to muscle growth.

Raised glutathionine levels helps increase strength and endurance. Those interested in physical fitness can benefit from a definite edge. (Journal of Applied Physiology 87: 1381-1385, 1999.)

Creatine Monohydrate – what would a weight lifting program be without mention of creating monohydrate, it works! And should always be included in every workout program from beginner to advanced.

The amino acid Leucine: Extra grams of leucine will help to boost the anabolic stimulus of proteins. By adding extra leucine to your protein rich meals, older athletes will build up more muscle protein. When your still 30 years old and below your body will still react well to the anabolic stimulus of protein rich meals, as you get older your sensitivity to the stimulus declines.

A leucine rich amino acid mix will strength the anabolic process in older athletes and help to support the catabolic process (break down of protein). Leucine supplements are gaining much popularity in the supplement field among strength and power athletes that are over 35 years old looking for that extra help in their anabolic process of muscle growth. <u>Adding at least 5 to 10 grams of leucine before your large protein meals of the day, adding two times a day of extra leucine on workout days will be most beneficial.</u>

(Sources – AM Journal of Physiology Endocrinol Metab. 2006 Auhust; 291(2):E381-7)

Abstract: A higher portion of leucine is required for optimal stimulation of the rate of muscle tissue protein synthesis by essential amino acids in the elderly; Christos S. Katsanos, Hisamine Kobayashi; Metabolism Unit, Shriners Burns Hospital, Galveston, Texas; Febuary 17 2006.

Chapter 4

<u>*Most Needed Supplements For Nutritional Workouts*</u>

The mainstay supplements that should be in every one's workout nutritional protocol should be the two different protein sources <u>fast & slow</u> utilized for different requirements thus creating a positive nitrogen balance priming your anabolic growth potential.

- "Hydrolyzed" protein powders from the recommended brands listed for each phenotype.
- The "Slow" digesting protein powders.
- The amino acid "Glutamine" taken on a daily basis. See brands recommended earlier.
- The branch chain amino acid "Leucine" or "BCCA's"
- Glutathionine – For muscle recovery and recuperation.

<u>**Note:**</u> *These supplements are your basic core nutrients that will help immensely in the growth of muscle tissue and aid in the recovery period. Other necessary supplements that help to increase growth hormone, testosterone, and insulin are also mentioned in*

later chapters in this book that you can pick and choose from as needed to further fuel your growth.

Choosing The Right Protein Powder

It's no secret that protein intake plays a very important role in building muscle and muscle repair. Choosing the correct protein powder is probably one of the most difficult choices most people have to make when they decide to  embark on a weight gaining regimen. With all the different kinds of protein powders available it is very easy to make the wrong choice to use per training to your particular needs on gaining muscle. Making the right choice can be a challenge for those wishing to make the correct decision.

This chapter will help shed some light on this topic to help you make the right decision on what type of protein powder will suit you best from the different protein powders to choose from:\

Whey protein isolate
Whey protein concentrate
Hydrolyzed whey
Calcium caseinate
Egg white
Whole egg
Micellar casein
Beef protein
Soy protein

Which protein is the best one to buy? What are the benefits? Which one has the highest protein per milligrams? These are some of the questions people mostly ask as make their choices in the health food stores.

We will break down the benefits of each protein and its proper use as far as muscle gains go and explain their best use during the different times of the day.

__Whey protein__ makes up 20% of the total milk protein. Whey is recognized for its excellent amino acid profile, high cysteine content, rapid digestion, and interesting variety of whey peptides. High quality whey protein powders are an excellent choice particularly for post-workout nutrition since they enter the blood stream rapidly to feed those depleted muscles just that were just worked out. Most of the whey protein powders that stock the supplement shelves are made up of whey concentrates mixed with small portions of whey isolates. Comparing the two, whey isolates is the more expensive protein powder than whey concentrate because it has a higher quality of protein (purer) and a higher biological value.

Whey protein isolates contain 90-98% protein while whey concentrate contains 7-80% protein. Whey protein isolate is the highest yield of protein currently available that comes from milk. It is easier absorbed and digested (within 1 hour) than whey concentrate.

Whey hydrolysates (also known as hydrolyzed whey protein, and peptides), are powerful proteins that are more quickly absorbed; more so than any other form of protein, since the body prefers peptides to whole proteins. High in essential and branch chain amino acids, hydrolysates are the most potentially anabolic for short term protein synthesis such as 15 minutes prior to a workout, during a workout, and immediately after a workout.

Casein protein makes up 80% of total milk protein. Casein is recognized for its excellent amino acid profile, slow digestion and interesting variety of peptides. Since casein is a slow digesting protein it is not used during workouts or after workouts. Casein is optimally used during any time of the day except breakfast and within 6 hours after a workout when your body requires a more immediate source. Bedtime would be an optimal choice here, and or when one will be away from a food source.

Micellar casein is a slow releasing protein and doesn't get the recognition as whey protein does. As a high protein product, casein is used as a food additive in dairy, dietary and baby foods. because of its slow digestion properties, casein provides a steady stream of amino acids to the muscles, long after whey proteins have dropped off. It has a biological value of 77. Whey is 104 and egg is 100. this number refers to the proportion of absorbed protein, more specifically the number of amino acids which can utilized by the body. Don't let caseins lower biological value fool you, it does have its advantages.

The main benefit of casein protein powder is that it's high in glutamine content. Out of all the protein powders, casein has the highest glutamine content, which can benefit you in building muscle and gaining weight by helping you preserve muscle mass and aiding the immune system. The other significant fact is more thorough absorption (7 hours) of amino acids by the body. Allowing the body to use the amino acids in a more efficient manner.

Protein Blends - are a mixture of various complete proteins, eggs, casein, whey concentrates, isolates, milk proteins, and soy. Using protein blends from various sources of protein help to create an anabolic environment helping you to get in a spectrum of different amino acids. Protein blends are great to use as a sustained source of protein or as a meal replacement.

Soy Protein Powder – made from soy beans and considered a complete protein comparable in quality to many of the animal based sources of protein. Low in saturated fat, powerful anti-oxidant properties that have been shown to lower cholesterol and help prevent heart disease. With a biological value of 94, easily digested and absorbed, soy is also high in the amino acid arginine, contains all the essential amino acids, it can serve the avid bodybuilder well in recovery and recuperation and rank up there with some of the best protein sources.

Egg Protein - Popularly known as the perfect protein that has been a staple food since years. With a biological value of 100, egg protein was a supreme source of protein before whey protein came along. Egg protein is considered a complete protein source having all the essential amino acids as well as nine non-essential amino acids. Scientists have used egg protein as the standard against which they judge all other proteins. Second only to mother's milk for human nutrition.

A big favorite among bodybuilding enthusiants and athletes all across the globe. Several years ago was consumed abundantly whether in its raw state or cooked at a dozen at a time, bodybuilders of old have made some of the best gains with the edible incredible egg. Rich in vitamins and essential minerals eggs will always be a staple choice in muscle building. Can be taken prior to workouts or after it will always be a sound and confident source of protein that you can't go wrong.

Advantages of using egg protein powders – it has a slower absorption rate (digested in 4 hrs) than whey protein. Virtually carbohydrate free making it an excellent choice if you are trying to stay lean. It is also good for those people that have allergies.

Beef Protein – A new choice among the protein filled supplement shelves, beef protein rich in creatine, minerals, and vitamins having a biological value of 90% and high in the amino acid alanine needed for the metabolism of glucose, allowing for the body to generate more fuel for an intense workout.

When choosing among the different protein sources, and considering the biological value and the absorption rate, one would have to decide which source of protein would benefit your cause of action. The fast proteins, the slow digesting proteins, and the mixed blends of protein sources. They each have their own use for what ever you need them to do, as far as gaining weight, losing weight or building muscle tissue.

Different protein sources have different digestion rates. Eggs and whey protein isolates have 100% absorption and then from there it starts to go down hill. Protein then is eventually broken down into amino acids. Its the efficiency of use where the amino acids do the most good in building muscle tissue.

Bioavailability of Protein Sources Index Score

Whey protein isolate blends - 100-159
Whey concentrate - 104
Whole Egg - 100
Cow's Milk - 91
Egg White - 88
Fish - 83
Beef - 80
Chicken - 79
Casein - 77
Rice -74
Soy - 59
Wheat - 54
Beans - 49
Peanuts – 43

Dollar for dollar, protein powders and meal replacement drinks tend to be more cost effective than whole food protein sources. But, they are still supplements, and the focus should still be on whole foods, and should be considered as the first choice. Whole foods can offer you a whole spectrum of nutrients that most powders can not. Most of your proteins should come from food choices, meats, Fish, poultry and eggs. Never let supplements take the place of whole foods.

The bottom line is to achieve optimal balance between whole foods and supplements. So what is the best protein to use? The answer is, there is no one best protein powder, using a combination of protein powders is actually your best choice. For the pre, during, and post workout phase you need to use the whey isolates or hydrolzed protein powders, or a combination of the two.

And if your looking for a strong protein powder to exploit your full growth potential during all times of the day then use a blend of protein powders. This will allow you to receive the full spectrum of amino acids receiving various rates of absorption from the different types of protein. Using a blend will create an anabolic environment from whey and an anti-catabolic environment from casein.

Supplements For Hormonal Manipulation: GH, Insulin & Testosterone To Further Your Muscle Building Response

Royal Jelly – (testosterone enhancer) I bet you didn't expect to find this natural Bee product here, did you?
This natural product from nature's busiest workers, is an all around product that helps your body combat stress induced resistance training; helps the body make testosterone, provides natural amino acids, vitamins, minerals, enzymes, and very high in vitamin B5, a natural cortisol suppressor, and is actually used by many health enthusiasts as an anti-aging supplement. Considered a nutritional power house! *But when purchasing make sure its kept cold or it will spoil. Pure 100% Royal Jelly can be a difference maker.*

Mucuna Prureins – (GH & Testosterone) an herbal testosterone releaser, GH stimulant, that is often used in the sports supplement market as an ergogenic aid in many testosterone and GH fomula's. High in natural L-dopa, which is typically extracted for those with Parkinson's Disease. Mucuna helps to boost your (GH) production and testosterone that can provide benefits in muscle recovery and growth. Good Products are from USP Labs "Powerful".

Alpha-GPC – (GH Enhancer) increases the ability of the pituitary gland to produce GH through acetylcholine release to act on cells to produce muscle growth. Often used with mucuna prureins in GH enhancing formula's.

Creatine Monohydrate (Myostatin Inhibitor) – found in high amounts in red meats, creatine has become a main stay product in the supplement world. Helping the body with energy production (ATP) and muscle cell dysplasia, can also be taken with your protein shakes to provide more of a muscle building kick.

Cordyceps Extract – (Testosterone Enhancer) used in traditional Chinese medicine for treating circulatory disorders and respiratory problems, cordyceps actually has amazing health benefits that will help you build muscle by also stimulating testosterone production as well. Although noted for its performance enhancing effect, endurance and strength, cordyceps is a supplement that you will benefit your training. Was also, once used by the Chinese field & track team during the Olympics when they shattered the world record. When buying, make sure its the extract and that its standardized for the highest percentage of polysaccharides to get maximum benefits from it. Is also becoming very popular among athletes for its endurance related abilities.

Mooyimo Extract (mumie) – (Hormone regulator) mooyimo is an exotic, effective, and until recently a secret enhancement product from the mountains of Russia. Mooyimo has been used by Russian athletes in the Olympics for decades. Rich in bioavailable fulvic, humic, and mineralized organic acids, thus making it the ultimate Adaptogen. Mooyimo has restorative and anabolic effects, including the activation of the anabolic process in different organs and systems (blood, liver, muscles, lymphatic system, central and peripheral nervous systems, skin, hair, and the gastrointestinal tract).

Mumie has become extremely popular with Russian and Eastern athletes allowing them them to train during periods of high intensity training and in recovery. Mumie can also be an effective at preventing age related-hormonal disorders, and so, it should be strongly considered as a nutrient for non-competitive athletes who participates in fitness programs. Mumie comes in as a highly recommended product for use by serious athletes and anyone else that participates in strenuous activities. Short term cycles of mumie is all that is needed by one looking to try the product, two weeks on one week off allows it to perform to its maximum level. Look for the extract version on line.

Colostrum – (GH & IGF-1 Enhancer) considered the first milk of human and animal life. Colostrum is a nutrient rich pre-milk that is secreted by the mammary glands of female mammals to nourish their young. Most often the colostrum is taken from the first 6 to 12 hours of the newborn's life. Colostrum contains the essential nutrients for a young cow to grow, develop and to sustain life. Bovine colostrum (cows) is practically identical to that of human colostrum; however bovine colostrum contains four times the amount of immune factors than that of human colostrum.

 Colostrum also is rich in growth factors, and immense amount of vitamins, minerals, and an abundance of amino acids, essential and non-essential. It is the fraction of growth factors, that help colostrum release an IgF-1 response, which helps to build lean muscle tissue that has become of interest to bodybuilders. Colostrum is slowly becoming a popular supplement with bodybuilders today, because of its extreme beneficial qualities in health and muscle building capabilities, a natural IgF-1 releaser that can make a difference in your health and muscle building capabilities. (*make sure the colostrum you buy is of the first 6-12 hours of delivery*).

Deer Antler Extract (IGF-1 & GH Enhancer) – velvet deer antler extract has been used in traditional Chinese medicine for over 2,000 years. It is known for its capabilities for improving everything from overall health and athletic performance. Clinical studies have shown that the IgF-1 found in deer antlers is capable of promoting muscle cell growth, connective tissue, bone, and nerve health. This is because deer antlers are considered as the fastest, natural growing tissue worldwide. This essential element contains more than 70 amino acids that are helpful in building muscle, and fighting the common symptoms of the aging process.

Now a days research scientists are conducting several studies and research works on the positive side of deer antler extract to humans. The deer antler extract for bodybuilding has shown an intense growth effects among athletes and bodybuilders. The ability of IgF-1 can stimulate the natural growth of muscles twice as powerful than any other supplements. Deer antler extract can help you build muscle faster, improve you recovery response, and benefit your overall health.

This supplement you can definitely feel working the first week of use, as I can attest to that myself. It just gets better week after week. Just make sure when buying you buy from a reliable source, as there are many counterfeiters out there. *A good one is from* ***"Max life Direct, Now, and Nutronics labs.com", you won't be disappointed!***

Tongkat Ali – (Testosterone Enhancer) this product comes from the island of Sumatra and is rapidly becoming depleted because of its capabilities in producing high amounts of testosterone.
You might want to consider this herbal product as a natural aphrodisiac, in which it is also primarily used as such in Sumatra, and in the rest of the world for its testosterone and aphrodisiac qualities.

This product is primarily used as an aphrodisiac, and as a treatment for erectile dysfunction in men. The bodybuilding community caught on about this herbal and realized that it increases testosterone quite significantly.

Tongkat Ali raises levels of testosterone four times the amount of what the body produces normally. But that's not all it does, it also inhibits *sex hormone binding globumin* (SHBG), thus assuring for more available free testosterone in the blood stream. It is this free testosterone that exerts its affect, not total testosterone in the blood stream, but its the free (available) testosterone that makes muscles grow. Tongkat can boost your testosterone back up to more youthful levels, increasing your capability to increase more muscle mass. ***Make sure when purchasing you get the Sumatran brand 200:1 extract and not the Indonisian one.***

MuscleMeds – (Methyl-Arimatest) (Testosterone Enhancer) a unique formula in that it functions as a testosterone booster and an anti-aromatase inhibitor keeping testosterone from metabolizing into estrogen. A cutting edge supplement from an excellent company that
delivers with results you can see and feel.

Bulbine Natalensis Extract – (Testosterone Enhancer & Aromatase Inhibitor) is a native herb from South Africa that may in small dosages substantially increase testosterone quickly, while at the same time reduce estrogen levels by 35%. This herb has recently been receiving a lot of attention from the press for its libido/testosterone boosting abilities. <u>Bulbine, seems to also be the only herbal extract that can raise testosterone and lower estrogen at the same time.</u> *When taking Bulbine, make sure to cycle it, 2 weeks on, 1 week off, and you also do not need large dosages, only a small amount is needed for its affects, more is not necessarily better when it comes to Bulbine. You also have to make sure when buying this extract, it is freeze dried.*

Suma Root extract – (Hormone regulator) a product of South America that has been used in Brazil as an aphrodisiac, a general tonic, and just a bout what ails the human body. Suma root is known for its content of (beta-ecdysterone) that has anabolic properties. Due to its anabolic action, suma root is now being used as a natural anabolic to build muscle and help treat chronic fatigue syndrome. Researched heavily by Russian scientists, it was known to contain 19 different amino acids, a large number of electrolytes, trace minerals, vitamins, and pantothenic acid (B5). It also contains a high amount of germanium that accounts for its ability as an oxygenator, and high source of iron content that may account for its traditional uses for anemia. The root also contains phyto chemicals that include saponins, pfaffic acid, glycosides, and nortriterpines. Suma was once called the "Russian Secret" because it was taken at one time by the Russian Athletes during the Olympic Games.

Suma's main anabolic action can be attributed to its high content of beta-ecdysterone and 3 novel ecdysteroid glycosides. Being a rich source of beta-edysterone that is the subject of a Japanese patent that was filed for a US patent in 1998 for a propriety extract of Suma (which extracted the ecdysterone and beta ecdysterone. These researchers claimed through various in vitro and vivo studies that compound maintained health and had other various health benefits as an overall tonic. Look for the highest standardized extract for beta-ecdysterones when buying Suma root.

Secretagogue GH-Releaser – *sold by MHP*, this (GH enhancer) works in helping the body produce more available growth hormone. Very popular among the anti-aging enthusiasts, for its anti-aging affects. This product is good for athletes and bodybuilders that are over 40 years old, as their GH production is dwindling downwards. A very effective product that you can actually feel working within weeks.

<u>**HGH Up** – **sold by "Applied Nutriceuticals"**,</u> this another (GH & testosterone) enhancing product that helps you to produce more GH, also an affective product that works equally well as the Secretagogue. Basically all have similar formula's and ingredients in so many of these GH Enhancers sold today. I'm just listing the ones that in my opinion work very well that I have tried myself that has some scientific merit behind it.

<u>**Prime** – **by USP Labs**,</u> (hormone regulator) Prime is an herbal formula that sells very

well for USP Labs that is sort a natural anabolic/adaptogen. Helps the body to promote thickness, size, and physical strength. Fly's off the shelf at vitamin stores!

Powerful – by USP Labs, this is a very potent (GH Releaser) that sells extremely well, and is usually sold out! Its main herb is the extract of "Mucuna Prureins" Velvet Bean, which has been the subject of multiple studies on growth hormone. Powerful has one of the strongest extractions of velvet bean on the market today for its L-dopa content, among GH enhancers sold today. You will literally feel it working within days, especially if your 40 years and older. Powerful also has another herbal compound from the herb Chlorophytum Boriviianum, that has specific Triterpene steroidal saponins and sapogonegins that boost the already power effect from the velvet bean extract, L-dopa. The formula sold today is a much more stronger one than what was sold last year. Reviews have been solid for this amazing product.

Pink Magic – *sold by USP Labs*, (Testosterone Enhancer) another fine product from USP Labs that is also very popular among the bodybuilders and gym enthsuiants. Pink magic is an herbal formula that consists of three powerful herbs in their own right, but when grouped together, you have a powerful combination with results that speak for itself. Pink Magic is kind of a testosterone booster with an adaptogenic affect that helps prevent catabolism within muscle tissue and provides more for an anabolic environment that's favorable for muscle growth.

Test Powder – (Testosterone enhancer) sold by USP labs, this is one of USP Labs newer products that just was recently introduced on the market, and I must say that the ingredients really interested me, that I am looking forward in trying it myself! The ingredients consist of an amino acid /herbal formula of "Mucuna Prureins" extract of 200mgs and D-Aspartic Acid, Trimethylglycine, Carnitine Tartrate, and several other ingredients as well, to me looks very promising as a well developed formula by a company that takes great pride in producing great products, and actually all of their products are great. Some of them have won supplement of the year. But based on USP Labs reputation I'm going to give this a try myself.

SuperCissus-RX - (Anabolic stimulator & Cortisol reducer) Another USP Lab product is one of my favorites that I personally always use on a consistent level. Cissus is an herb from India that has amazing anabolic properties for strengthening tendons, and ligaments. It has won supplement of the year for that reason. This patent pending product has quickly established itself among customers and industry insiders alike. It has won numerous awards as the #1 joint product of the year for 2008 and 2009. They key ingredient is "Cissus Quandrangularis" that has been supported by centuries of use in Ayuredic Traditional Medicine in India, it has also been the subject of numerous clinical studies.

Great to use for nagging joint related problems and trouble area's of the body from stress induced bodybuilding. Its anabolic affect for muscle building properties can be compared to the steroid "D-Ball" Dianabol. With that, enough said! This is one product that you shouldn't be without.

HumanoGrowth – *from Labrada Nutrition*, Humanogrowth is a cutting edge embryonic peptide matrix (standardized chicken embryo extract) developed in Eastern Europe, designed to help the body support testosterone production and decrease recovery time. Humanogrowth contains naturally occurring growth factors that have a unique bio-stimulating properties; like IGF-1,IGF-2,FGF- Fibroblast growth factors, NGF-Nerve growth factors, EGF- Embryo growth factors, and CTGF -Connective tissue growth factors. Humanogrowth is not your ordinary testosterone-booster, but a highly developed cutting edge supplement that is geared to help your body produce growth promoting fractions that stimulate muscle tissue growth and increase your recovery time for complete recuperation. This a supplement that you stay on and the results are kind of accumulative. Again a good product for muscle building.

Tribulus Terrestris Extract – Bulgarian tribulus is a quality testosterone booster that has been made very popular quickly by the Bulgarian Olympic Weightlifting team years ago, and to which is still very popular today. Tribulus must be bought in a high quality extract standardized for its steroidal saponins, the percentage of saponins should be 40% or higher if you are going to see results. Tribulus has a *unique ability in increasing levels of (LH) leutenizing hormone which in turn spurs significant increases in the levels of testosterone*. In addition to its testosterone boosting affect, There were two solid tribulus studies suggesting that it was also found to be a nitric oxide stimulator.

Nitric oxide can significantly impact muscle contractiblity and nutrient metabolism. Tribulus is also found in many of the testosterone boosting formula's on the market today, because it works!

Androtest – rated as the industries protodioscin content leader, androtest is another herbal formula that has powerful testosterone boosting capabilities to help build muscle. The formula consists of two of the most natural potent testosterone producing herbs, Tribulus is one of the ingredients in androtest that is standardized to 40% to 48% protodioscin, and Tongkat Ali being the other powerful active ingredient standardized for its quassinoid content.

Androtest impressively, in one clinical study increased levels of DHEA by 47%, SHBG decreased by 66% and the free available testosterone index escalated by 73%. This new generation of protodioscin-rich tribulus, and Tongkat Ali represent what may be the single most potent and natural testosterone producing supplement on the market today. Look for androtest on the Prosource.net site on the internet.

Leucine - is known for its capacity to stimulate insulin release and the role insulin has on modulating leucine's effect on protein synthesis and most importantly how these effects can be manipulated for optimization of protein balance. This branched chain amino acid appears to be the primary regulator of protein synthesis. The three major components of protein balance studied include include leucine, insulin, and exercise.

Adding this branch chain amino acid to your training regimen, 5 to 10 grams several times day along with your protein meals or shake, will surely induce a positive anabolic environment towards your muscle development. Leucine plays a prominet role in muscle loss with aging athletes, adding it back in sufficient amounts will bring back your muscles to youthful levels. And by adding glutamine and BCAA's will further advance the muscle building response of Leucine.

CHAPTER 5

Performance Pre-Workout Supplements To Consider

1. **USP Labs – (Jack-3d Micro)** – (endurance enhancer) A company that always produces top of the line quality and products that deliver. Jack3dMicro is a new pre-workout formula of the previous Jack3d, has some very interesting ingredients that I'm kind of excited about and looking forward in trying myself, I'm a big follower of the USP labs line for their great formulated products that have never failed. This one looks like a keeper!

2. **USP Labs – (Jack3d)** - excellent formula that you can feel working right from the first serving. (great feedback from this product) (Same as above)

3. **MHP's (NO-BOMB)** - A good nitric oxide enhancer, This is another quality company that gets good reviews from their product line. NO-BOMB is a revolutionary nitric oxide booster that will give you incredible muscle pumps, sustained energy and strength. The formulation of this product is a sound one with ingredients you can feel working.

4. **MHP – (TRAC Extreme)** – a powerful formula that really boosts the nitric oxide level to where you can get awesome muscle pumps and energy that keeps you going without feeling that wired jittery feeling. Trac is a product that works very well! Loaded with nutrients making this a powerfull pe-workout formula.

5. **Gaspari Nutrition -(Super Pump Max)** – a pre-workout supplement that

produces skin tearing pumps, great reviews! Packed with branched amino acids, nitric oxide boosters, electrolytes, creatine, and nutritional co-factors. The Gaspari line is also another reputable company that poduces quality products.

6. **BPI-Sports (1.M.R.)** - (Nitric Oxide booster) BPI Sports supplement line is relatively new product line has been getting some great reviews lately. Excellent company with products that deliver results. I have personally tried some of them with great satisfaction. Provides the user with a sustained amount of energy and pumps without that jittery feeling which most pre-workout supplements give.

7. **Gaspari Nutrition -(Vasotropin)** - (Nitric Oxide booster) Advertised as the "Ultimate Pump Solution" this formula utilizes some high-tech nutritional ingredients that promises top deliver sustained energy levels with unbelievable pumps. Expensive product, but the Gaspari line of supplements are backed by research and has never produced a non-quality product.

8. **Millennium Sports Technologies – (Cordygen 5)** - (Endurance enhancer) A patented formula that incorporates a blend of 5 strains and 4 species of the cordyceps mushroom extract 100% USDA certified organic and highly concentrated in a time-released formula. Cordyceps helps you maximize oxygen utilization for sustained levels of endurance and muscular strength. Cordygen 5 is used by the top athletes around the world for its ability in increasing oxygen utilization, strength, endurance, and sustained energy levels. (One of my personal favorites).

9. **Millennium Sports Technologies – (Ultra Cordygen Vo2)** same as above but new and improved, super potent! Maximizes oxygen utilization, decreases oxygen debt, maximizes endurance, increases Vo2 max, and increases ATP production.

10. **BSN – (Hyper FX)** a very good company that caters to bodybuilding supplements. Hyper FX is a good pre-workout supplement that is packed with nutrition. (Nitric Oxide booster)

11. **CytoSports – (CytoMax)** this is an exercise and ***recovery drink*** formulated with an advanced complex carbohydrate, electrolyte performance and recovery drink. CytoMax ensures you to stay positively hydrated, steady energy levels, and helps you to minize post exercise muscle soreness. Cytomax also helps to buffer lactic-acid production in muscle tissue allowing you to train longer and recovery quickly. Great pre-workout supplement!

12. **Athletic Edge Nutrition -(IntraXcell)** this a beta-alanine formula that's been backed by major university, peer reviewed studies performed on humans, not the

typical cell or rat studies upon many other manufactures generally base claims on. Beta-Alanine has been shown to boost muscular strength, muscular anaerobic endurance, increase aerobic endurance, and increase exercise capacity so you could train harder and longer.

13. **Metabolic Nutrition – (C.G.P.)** creatine glycerol phosphate, a new patented creating formula that is able to accelerate absorption in the G.I. Tract via a specialized pathway

that eliminates all the negative side effects associated with most creatine products. C.G.P. Serves as its own high energy phosphate and electrolyte reservoir contributing to the production of ATP, delaying fatigue, increasing strength, and magnifying endurance.

14. *__Applied Nutraceuticals – (Lit-Up)__* this product utilizes the most cutting edge formulation that yields cumulative results in that it increases energy levels, testosterone, and functions as a anticatabolic, suppressing cortisol and increases the mind to muscle connection.

CHAPTER 6

Boosting Your Hormones For Maximum Muscle Development Through Diet & Exercises

There are several ways that we can increase our own levels of testosterone and growth hormone, through natural means without resorting to steroids. One way is by employing certain basic exercise movements, and the best exercise's are compound movements using multiple muscle groups. Examples of this would be – *squats, bench press, rowing, dead lifts, pull ups, and power cleans.*

There are also a couple of things to keep in mind – **Focus on lower body exercises like squats,** that can provide a healthy flow of these powerful hormones in a way the upper lifts won't.

Focus on power – making sure that you are focusing on power when you are trying to add size to your frame. Mix up also your sets and reps to cover both the high and low rep counts. But be sure to add power sets in there with lower reps of 3-5 with higher weight added to it. Try at least one to two times a week for a max lift in bench press, dead lifts, power cleans, or high pulls. **Here are four power exercises that will boost your testosterone and GH levels: and add some serious muscle mass.**

1. **Dead lifts** – This exercise is a must that needs to be in your workout program if you want to add size fast, and build strength.(keep the bar close to your body and focus lifting with your legs, get low and don't let your knees, chest, or face lean forward beyond your toes as your lifting the bar up. Keeping the back straight.

Dead-Lifts

2. <u>**Power Squats**</u> – Will help you increase your over all size by naturally boosting your testosterone and GH much like dead lifts can. When performing power squats make sure no part of your body leans forward past your toes, keep your eyes position squating your

SQUAT

focused on looking up at your eye level from your starting point as you begin down making sure that your buttocks touch ankles on the down ward part of the movement.

3. <u>**Power Cleans**</u> – this is considered an Olympic lift that will add size, power and strength to your over all body, and may be the best over all exercise that one never adds to their program. A great hormone booster because of it being an explosive movement. To perform this movement, begin by crouching over the Olympic bar hand grip should be a bout shoulder level, with knees bent slightly and your back more or less parallel to the floor. As you pull the weight past your knees, straighten your body and pull it up to your shoulder position as if you were going to perform a military press. (for those that are not sure how to perform this movement, you tube has excellent video's on this and many other Olympic movements).

Power Cleans

4. <u>Barbell Bench Press</u> – when done in the power lifting method, you are doing 1 rep maximum for your greatest amount of weight that you can handle. Trying to complete about 3-5 sets of each. Finish off with medium to light weight on the bar and perform as many reps as you can, then strip off some more weight and perform the max reps as you can do with minimum rest, that is the key for hormonal stimulation.

Barbell Bench Press

By knowing how to increase testosterone through certain exercises, we can have the added advantage of manipulating our hormones to build muscle tissue. By performing compound movements with brief high intensity sessions, your body responds by providing short spurts of hormone release, be it testosterone or GH. Heavy weight with 4-6 reps and high intensity sessions are the best in boosting testosterone. Now endurance training on the other hand has a different hormonal effect. It leads to increased "cortisol levels" and low testosterone levels, and that we do not want as cortisol is a catabolic hormone.

So, training for long extended periods is detrimental to your testosterone and Gh levels. Workouts should last no more than 45 minutes to an hour at most. Your natural levels of testosterone will peak at 45 minutes into an intense weight training workout. You really do not need to train for longer periods than that, if you workout hard, you will get the results you looking for.

Your diet also plays an important role in boosting your testosterone levels. An extremely low carb and low fat diet will actually decrease your testosterone. Keep healthy carbs and essential fats in your diet, and eat plenty of quality protein.

CHAPTER 7

Boosting Your Testosterone Levels Through Diet For Natural

Muscle Growth

Add healthy monounsaturated fats like olive oil to your daily diet to help get your daily requirements of up to 35% to 50%, which boosts testosterone. ***(Research by Volek et al.)***

Concluded in their findings that monounsaturated fats and saturated fat dramatically raised testosterone levels by 62% and 59% respectively. <u>Monounsaturated fats like olive oil, canola oil, nuts, peanut butter, and avocados.</u> Moreover foods high in healthy omega 3 fatty acids would be a great source of testosterone raising fats. <u>With the best source of omega 3 being fatty fish like herring, mackeral, sardines, tuna, and salmon.</u>

Omega 3's are also found in plant foods walnuts, pumpkin seeds, flax seeds, and flax seed oil. By keeping your consumption of monounsaturated oils and omega 3's up around 35% to 50%, which is the amount research shows to be optimal for raising your testosterone levels.

In addition to healthy fats and Omega 3's for increasing testosterone levels, meat and diary products also are "key" ingredients in any diet based on raising your testosterone levels. The foods listed below are testosterone boosting foods:

- **<u>Meats</u>** – a great source of protein, fats, minerals (zinc & iron), and vitamins. Make sure your cuts of meat are of lean variety. Some of the best cuts of meat for a low carb (higher-fat0 approach to building muscle, the top choices are:

- ***Sirloin*** – 23.6 grams of protein, 13 grams of fat, 219 calories.
- ***Chuck meat*** – 23.2 grams of protein, 20 grams of fat, 282 calories.

For a high protein low-fat option:

- ***Round*** – 25.6 grams of protein, 8.1 grams of fat, 183 calories. (*Round meat is the highest in protein and also the lowest in fat*)

- **<u>The incredible Egg</u>** (*A Protein Revelation*) – A bodybuilders best friend. Eggs have been valued by bodybuilders since bodybuilding evolved. Always a gold standard by which all other proteins are measured with a *PDCAAS (Protein Digestibility Corrected Amino Acid Score)* score of number 1 – the highest value possible – it has a *BV (biological value) of 100* and a highly balanced amino acid profile. Meaning your body can not find a protein source with a better conversion rate to muscle turn over!

Not surprisingly, given egg's status as a first line of muscle building food, egg protein as a supplement can be used by anyone in need of a high quality protein to meet daily needs of important muscular growth. It may be just what you need to reach your physique goals. Popularized by the great nutritional guru's Vince Gironda, and Rheo H. Blair in the golden era of bodybuilding, the 60's.

The elements in eggs have been prized for their anabolic activity full of muscle building nutrients, with a high quality protein source lactose-free, containing arachidonic acid, follistatin (natural myostatin inhibitor), TGF beta proteins, vitamins, minerals, and fatty acids. Egg yolks contain significant concentrations of follistatin, a natural myostatin antagonist (blocker) that inhibits muscle growth and is the most potent powerful inhibitor of muscle growth to date!

(References- Journal of American College, Vol 25, No. 5, Abstract 66, October 2006) (Follistatin complexes Myostatin and antagonises Myostatin levels' Colker C)

Fertile egg yolks contain significant amounts of follistatin. Now fortified with omega 3 fatty acids. One of the most unworthy and foolish things to do is throwing away the egg yolks and eating only the white part of the egg. Why? A misconception that has given the nutritious part of the egg yolk a bad rap because of the cholesterol content which is foolish. Studies also show that the cholesterol found in eggs is not harmful. Eggs are rich in lecithin and lecithin is a natural emulsifier. Try and make sure you get in 3 to 4 eggs in your daily diet. Egg yolks are very rich in Lecthin and choline, and contains 90% of the fat soluble vitamins and essential fatty acids. Lecithin helps to dissolve and liquify cholesterol, choline is helpful for liver health and functioning.

During the golden years of bodybuilding, Larry Scott, Sergio Olivia, Freddie Prinze, Dave Draper, and Arnold the great all would eat eggs like it was going out of style! Eggs were the primary bodybuilding anabolic food along side of milk, steaks, and chicken. It was not uncommon for these great bodybuilders of their time to eat a dozen or so of eggs on a daily basis.

Back then that was their primary sort of protein powder that they would chug down either in its raw state, scrambled, or sunny side up. Considered a complete food and provides a healthy muscle building diet, especially for bodybuilders. Eggs contain about 6 to 7 grams of high quality protein per egg, so high that it is often used as the standard by which other foods are measured. They contain vitamin A, E and K and a range of B vitamins such as B12 (energy), B2, and folic acid. Eggs also contain all of the eight essential amino acids need for optimal muscle growth and recovery, and minerals like iron, calcium, and zinc.

The white part of the egg contains no fat what so ever, and the yolk contains about 5 grams of saturated fat, but only a small portion of this is saturated fat, about 1.6 grams. Eggs do contain cholesterol which is nullified or emulsified by the lecithin content that is normally found in the yolk. It is also generally accepted that the dietary cholesterol does not raise blood cholesterol levels from whole eggs. Bodybuilders or those seeking to bulk up muscle are in particular need for fat in foods at a time when they have a high energy requirement for growth but limited appetites.

Make eggs part of your anabolic food cycle and reap the health producing muscle growth benefits it provides you in a natural way.

- **Oysters** - a great source of testosterone boosting minerals, especially "zinc" which is required in the metabolism of testosterone. Consuming oysters (raw) at least once a week, is known to make a huge difference in testosterone stimulation.

- **Nuts** – almonds, cashews, walnuts, peanuts, are some very essential foods in boosting testosterone levels. Also a great nutritious snack in between meals.

- **Beans** – packed with proteins and zinc are also known to be great testosterone enhancers. Which include soy beans, chick peas, black beans, and kidney beans. They are also low in fat and high in fiber. Ensure that you include a variety of beans in your diet.

- **Dairy** - get your glass of milk daily, whether it be from skimmed or low fat milk, also include with that yogurt and cottage cheese (high glutamine content).

- **Fruits** – there are specific fruits that contain necessary ingredients that are vital in testosterone production, and they include bananas, figs, avocados, and all the different types of berries. By making a nutritious fruit smoothie with skimmed milk, you will enjoy a power house drink that will give you all the energy and testosterone boosting nutrients you'll need.

(References- The 4-Hour Body by Timothy Ferris)

CHAPTER 8

Essential Fatty Acid's

Essential fatty acids are important nutrients that your body needs to be able to function normally in the manufacture of its hormones, they are called essential for a good reason. The body can not manufacture them and we must get them through our diet. In bodybuilding and weightlifting essential fatty acids are a basic requirement in assisting our muscle growth and for the production of testosterone and other vital hormones.

Research shows that there is large amounts of evidence that shows essential fats are necessary for countless metabolic functions from, healthy brain function, fat metabolism, healthy sex drive, and the manufacture of human hormones.

The popularity of essential fatty acids is growing on a steady pace and bodybuilders are beginning to understand the value they bring in muscle growth and repair. It is absolutely necessary that we get these fatty acids through our diet on a daily basis. Certain foods are high in the Omega 3's and omega 6 like – *meats, avocado's, olive oil, fish, flax seeds, nuts, seeds and eggs* are all excellent dietary sources of essential fatty acids. Supplementing with a good essential fatty acid supplement makes good sense in making sure your getting the necessary omega 3's. Essential fatty acid supplements come in a variety of ways - from gel caps, powders, granules, and liquids. Choose one that will fit your needs and watch your muscles take off with new growth.

Popular Essential Fatty Acid Supplements

Barlean's Organic Oils - Barleans Flax Seed Oil

Spectrum Natural's – Ground Organic Flax Seed

Source Natural's – Krill Oil

Health From The Sun – Omega 3-6-9

Flora – Udo's Choice Oil Blend

Labrada Nutrition – EFA Lean Gold Gel Caps

CHAPTER 9
Branch Chain Amino Acid's (BCAA's)

Overview:

Leucine, valine, and isoleucine are what is known as the branch chain amino acids. These in my opinion are the most beneficial and effective supplements in any sports nutritional supplement program. They make up 35% of your muscle tissue and are considered the building blocks of the body. They must be present for molecular growth to take place. These specific amino acids directly influence protein metabolism and synthesis.

They support the immune system, reduce fatigue, diminish post exercise muscle soreness, prevent muscle protein breakdown and are anticatabolic. Branch chain amino acids are very widely used in sports nutrition to enhance muscular growth, and stimulate the anabolic pathways.

The proper dose in taking branch chain amino's is 5 to 10 grams before a workout and 5 to 10 grams after. If increased performance is needed for recovery and soreness, you can increase the dosage to 10 to 20 grams before and 10 to 20 grams after a workout. Also by taking them with a post recovery meal or protein shake it will help to speed things up as far as muscle growth and repair is concerned.

One thing of importance that bares mention for older athletes, 30 plus, is that Leucine can benefit older bodybuilders above 30 years old by helping to increase protein synthesis.. When your below 30 your body reacts well to the anabolic stimulus of a protein-rich meal. But, as you get older, your sensitivity to the stimulus declines. Supplementing your diet with extra grams of Leucine will increase the production of insulin and stimulate the molecular capability of muscle cells to build up muscle fiber. *According to American scientists in the Journal of Physiology, Endocrinology & Metabolism; 2006 August; 291(2):E381-7.*

Leucine as a supplement will inhibit the breakdown of muscle mass. Adding it to your protein shakes containing additional carbs will boost your muscle protein synthesis production. Leucine only works if you use it in combination with proteins and amino acids. If you consume it on its own, or in combination with carbs it has no effect

(J Strength Cond Res. 2010 Aug; 24(8): 2211-9).

Popluar BCAA's Brands To Take

Optimum Nutrition -Mega BCAA's

USP Labs – Modern BCAA's

Labrada - BCAA Power

MHP – BCAA 3000

Inner Power – BCAA Peak

Pro Lab Nutrition – BCAA Plus

Leucine by All Max Nutrition.

According to the studies taken, doses of Leucine as high 20 grams may be the most effective range to induce the anabolic effect of Leucine based on the findings of researchers at the *University of Nottingham published in the Journal of Nutrition in 2006.* Earlier studies had suggested a minimum dose of 3 grams for healthy people and probably a higher intake for elderly people. Bodybuilders have started taking doses of 5-8 grams of Leucine since then. Based on these findings most bodybuilders have done fairly well on doses of 5 to 10 grams several times a day.

Combined with other amino acids like branched chain amino acids and/or Glutamine will make for a potent anti-metabolic blend to increase strength, muscle mass, and recovery. Make sure you take it with your protein shake, BCAA's, and Glutamine.

CHAPTER 10

Over Training 101: What You Need To Know

How does one know that their over training? When some people train 5 to 6 days a week and perform 8 to 10 sets per body part on full body workouts, that's over training. You have to realize that there are so many training programs out there and so many of them contradict one another its ridiculous, and its know wonder that so many beginners over train right from the get go thinking that their on their way to muscle growth.

I'm sure you get the picture, <u>but basically over training is where you train your body above its capacity and it can not recover and adapt quickly enough for your next training session</u>. Which means that your training too hard with not enough rest and recuperation, or hydration. A good note to go by when training is when one finishes their training sessions and can still train for an additional half hour. You should never finish your training session on the last set and rep of your training program feeling very tired. That is the first sighn that your beginning to feel the effects of over training. Always finish strong with energy still left in your tank.

Symptoms of Over-Training: Overview

With me through the years of being a personal trainer & coach, I've noticed the symptoms quite easily. For one, when you see the same individual day in and day out training in the gym along side of you through the weeks and months, and they basically look the same. You kind of know that something is wrong here? Also the big factor for me was they would be at the gym before me and still be there trying to finish up their workouts, and in the mean time, I'm done and hitting the showers already, you get the picture?

But here are the most common symptoms of over training;

you just can not seem to get any bigger after weeks and months of training.

your energy levels die out in the middle of workouts.

your muscles are always sore the next day following your workouts.

you have a general lack of energy that seems to never go away.

your sleeping habits are off, and never quite feel that you slept enough.

you just don't seem to get motivated for your next workouts.

Seems obvious doesn't? if you have any of these symptoms then your over training and failing to make the gains that you need to make and look the way you want to.

If your training correctly you should feel energized and always looking forward to your next workout day. You should also be making steady and consistent gains on a monthly basis. <u>That right there should make one realize that something is wrong with your training.</u>

Your workouts should always feel progressive and positive on a weekly basis as well. If your diet is correct and your getting enough of the protein your body requires, taaking the proper supplements, and sleeping correctly. Then you should be able to make all the gains you need providing all of the above.

Often at times, over training can happen to the best of us, even experienced bodybuilders go through it. If that's the case it always best to just shut it down and take a week or two off and just regroup allowing your body a complete recovery period. Come back with a new strategy.

I myself will apply this practice, because at times we as experienced bodybuilders fail to realize that after say six to ten months of training, we forget to take a break of a week to two weeks off. For some people this can be a great thing as it just brings on new growth once you start again with your training.

That's always a good idea, taking breaks after so many months of working out. It sort of brings a new sense of enthusiasm to the table. Taking two week breaks gives your muscles a break and yourself a chance to re-evaluate your progress thus far, and to either modify or change certain things of your training or diet, supplements, etc.

I have always made great progress when I started to take rest periods of a week or so and often noticed just by doing that I've gotten bigger in size. Now that's a good thing when that happens, isn't it?

So in reality, the best person to design your muscle building routine is you! With of course some help with what I've given you here in this book!

Over Training Syndrome: How to Avoid it

Over training occurs when athletes train far and above their recovery process not allowing the body to recuperate properly. This is a common practice with so many novice and well advanced athletes thinking that more is necessarily better. Which is not the case, as too much overload and or too little recovery just leads to training regimen's that can backfire and lead to no progress at all in regards to muscle growth. Bodybuilding and weightlifting requires a balance between over load and recovery, and here in this chapter we will deal with how to avoid over training syndrome the proper way.

While there are many proposed ways to objectively test for over training, the most accurate and sensitive way are measurements in your psychological demeanor, symptoms and signs as your change of mental state, decreased positive feelings in your sport, fatigue, depression and failure to make bodybuilding progress which usually appears after a few days of intense training. Here are some of the most common symptoms to help you better distinguish over training syndrome.

Over Training Signs and Symptoms On The Nervous System

1. Early onset of fatigue during training.
2. Weak appetite.
3. Trouble sleeping
4. Irritability.
5. Depression.
6. Weight loss.
7. Increased metabolic rate.

Over Training Effects on Hormone Levels

1. Decreased levels of testosterone.
2. Decreased Thyroid hormone levels.
3. Increased levels of Cortisol.
4. Decreased levels of Growth hormone.

The increased levels of cortisol along with decreased levels of testosterone are a deadly combination as this leads to muscle tissue breakdown, which will ultimately lead to muscle loss. There are many studies that have indicated the body's hormonal response in regards to over training affects the whole body and that it can have a serious affect in your muscle building process.

The best treatment for over training is simply to just rest! How much rest you need depends on on how long you've been in this cycle, but generally sometimes its just better to take a week or two off from training and allow for a complete recovery. Use the time off to go over your training routine and see where you may have done too many exercises per certain body parts, reevaluate where you may have over done it. Take additional nutritional supplements that may help you in sustaining your energy level and give your recovery process a jolt that will help prevent future cycles of over training. Supplements like **"Glutathione"** can help prevent over training tremendously by strengthening your immune system. The amino acid **Glutamine** can combat the various stresses brought on by heavy training.

Supplementing with Glutamine has been shown to keep the body in a positive nitrogen balance as well as combat excess cortisol which is a big plus. Given Glutamine's low cost availability, it would be of great benefit to include this amino acid in your training program. Glutamine can be a great anabolic aid in that it prevents excess cortisol and muscle wasting syndrome. I generally take 10 to 30 grams of Glutamine myself and can honestly say it has helped me a great deal.

You may also want to look into some herbal cortisol inhibitors like **Ashwaganda, Schizandria, Rhodeola Rosea, and Phosphitadyserine**. Cortisol is catabolic to muscle tissue and excess levels will hinder your muscle building efforts to a stand still. These supplements will help keep your cortisol levels down allowing you a wide open path to muscle growth.

Overview: Solutions in Combating Over Training Syndrome

1. Take a break from training to allow time for recovery.
2. Reevaluate your training program, by reducing the volume of exercises and time spent in the gym.
3. Make sure your getting enough sleep and rest for adequate recuperation.
4. Massage the affected muscles, and take a cold to hot shower to stimulate hormonal release.
5. Ensure that your caloric intake and protein matches that of your expenditure during training sessions.
6. Address your training with supplementation designed to combat excess stress placed on muscles during intense exercise's. Utilizing supplements listed above.
7. Learn to change your weightlifting programs around never doing the same movements for months at a time to prevent boredom.
8. Shock your muscles with different training principles, as muscle can get complacent if doing the same type of routine over and over again.
9. Make *Glutathionine, and Glutamine* part of your supplement routine to help prevent over training.

CHAPTER 11

Cortisol & It's Implications On Muscle Growth

<u>Cortisol, is a bodybuilders worst nightmare for muscle-building.</u> Cortisol is termed catabolic as it has the opposite effect to testosterone, insulin and growth hormone (GH) in that it breaks down muscle tissue. Cortisol is released by the adrenal glands in response to mental and physical stress. It is also the body's primary catabolic hormone. It is therefore essential that levels of cortisol do not go in excess, as otherwise it can lead you to a muscle building halt.

<u>It is the excess levels that concern us that is problem for bodybuilders, not cortisol itself.</u> However, your body does require cortisol to maintain important processes during prolonged periods of stress. Without cortisol, you would go into shock and die if exposed to severe trauma. But for some reason our own bodies just don't know when to quit producing it when agitated or stimulated. Excess levels that are not under control can cause a range of health problems which are:

- **Reduce the output of GH and testosterone.**
- **Reduce muscle tissue and cause abdominal fat.**
- **Can cause an imbalance of blood sugar levels.**
- **Impair memory and learning**
- **Impair immunity levels.**
- **Can cause disease's such as Cushing's Syndrome.**

Although cortisol release can not be prevented, it can be controlled through dietary means and with supplementation. Cortisol is at it's highest during the morning hours in preparing the body for on-coming day, and it is also at it's lowest during night time when we are sleeping. Certain beverages that have caffeine are soda's, coffee, and the super high energy drinks that they sell commercially.

One study showed that individuals with too much cortisol found it impossible to lose weight even with the perfect diet and exercise program. Another important factor to consider is over training and spending pro-longed hours in the gym. This can only negate all the hard work spent in the gym trying to build muscle.

So by having excess levels of cortisol, an athlete is at a great disadvantage in trying to successfully build muscle tissue. As for weight training the more the intense the exercises are, the higher the release of cortisol will be. But The more experienced athletes or bodybuilders are in training often show little or no change in cortisol output. Because they have adapted, some by intensifying their workouts to an hour or less. University studies done on weightlifting and athletes showed cortisol release to be at it's highest at one hour of weightlifting resistance training. Some signs of excess cortisol production in the body are; water retention, excess fat in the central area of the body like the stomach and buttocks, and the failure to increase in muscle growth and strength.

Cortisol also promotes the release of **"*Myostatin*"**, a protein that breaks down muscle tissue.

Signs of inadequate levels of cortisol are weakness and fatigue. Cortisol also has an inverse relationship with testosterone, growth hormone, and insulin. When cortisol levels are high, it depresses the effects of these other anabolic hormones.

Over Training and Cortisol: How It Affects Muscle Growth

For those of you who are looking to add muscle growth and strength, cortisol is the one hormone that you should be familiar with. Classified as a catabolic steroid, referring to the break down of muscle tissue, cortisol will also play a role in increasing body fat and water retention. Cortisol also has an inverse relationship with the anabolic hormones, insulin, testosterone, and growth hormone. The higher your cortisol levels the lower these three anabolic hormones are. Steroids help to induce muscle growth by counter acting cortisol levels in muscle tissue.

Cortisol release is set off by various types of stress, which includes exercising, over training, life style, etc.

By the time i realized that i was way over training generating excess cortisol myself, thinking that more is better, and in reality less is better when it comes to muscular growth. As i soon discovered this concept, I changed a few things in my training sessions, and added some cortisol blockers, I finally then began to make some head way, and wow, what a difference. I spent less time in the gym about 45 minutes to an hour at most, and lowered my sets and reps, exercises per body parts, and then boy did my gains accelerate!

Cortisol Overview:

To increase muscle mass you need to adhere to, that all aspects of bodybuilding and lifestyle are completely balanced. That means you are consuming a proper diet pertaining to your particular needs as a bodybuilder, your also doing just enough training sets, reps, taking the necessary precautions of blocking cortisol, and keeping well hydrated.

All these factors play a big part in developing your muscular growth. The most import factor to consider that can hinder muscular growth is cortisol. You have to realize also that just about any type of intense training can bring on the release of cortisol, and athletes with the highest levels of cortisol are bodybuilders, due to their over all training sessions.

Cortisol is triggered by a stress response, it can be through a mental type of stress or physical. <u>Your body does not know the difference</u>. Considered a catabolic hormone, meaning it eats muscle tissue and can stop you from making any positive muscle gains, But yet its still a necessary and vital hormone that we need to survive and function well physiologically.

Cortisol can not also be totally eliminated from the body, as it is needed to maintain important processes during prolonged bouts of stress. But as it pertains to bodybuilding, cortisol will reduce the body's ability to process amino acids and build muscle. We just need to find the right balance.

Excess levels of cortisol will also inhibit growth hormone levels by stimulating the release of growth hormone antagnostics. As powerful as cortisol is, there are ways to control it for our particular needs in bodybuilding. The **_first step_** is to make sure we get enough sleep each day, because a lack of sleep is basically a signal to the body that there is some form of stress going on here.

The **_second step_** is to not over train during each of your workout sessions. <u>More is not necessarily better.</u> But that doesn't mean to not put enough intensity in your workouts either, because muscle is torn down while we workout, but grows when we rest up providing we cover the necessary steps.

Third, eliminate certain unnecessary trigger points that activated cortisol, like too much caffiene in your daily diet, coffee, soda's, and lifestyle stressors.

Fourth, introduce supplements that help with balancing cortisol levels like herbal adaptogens mentioned in this book.

Supplements That Help To Control Cortisol Levels

Vitamin-C **– a study done in the 90's showed that weightlifters taking extra vitamin - c boosted their cortisol to testosterone ratio by 20%.

Vitamin B5 & B2 **– needed by the adrenal glands to manufacture adrenal hormones that helps to balance cortisol levels.

Cissus Quadrangularis*** – (Super Cissus RX by Usp labs) Was shown to inhibit cortisol by 32% stronger than the anabolic steroid deca-durobolin in studies. **_(Indian J Med res. 1964 mar 52; 279:91) (see ergo-log.com)_**

Phosphatidyserine*** – 300 mgs two times per day lowered cortisol levels by 15-30%.

Rhodiola Rosea – a great adaptogen that helps to keep stress levels under control and calms the mind.

Magnolia Bark ** – an effective herb that is used to control anxiety and stress which therefore helps lowering cortisol.

Royal Jelly ** – very high in vitamin B5 that is specific in producing adrenal stress hormones.

DHEA ** – a natural hormone of the adrenal glands that declines after the age 30 seems to have some powerful anti-cortisol effects.

L-Glutamine *** – the most abundant amino acid in the muscle tissue that research suggests that glutamine levels may be a good indicator of over training. Glutamine directly prevents the cortisol induced degradation of muscle tissue wasting.

Siberian Ginseng * – used extensively by Russian and Asian athletes to combat cortisol levels prior to training.

Ashwaganda ** – a powerful adaptogen used for stress control and the over-production of cortisol.

Horny Goat Weed **– studies have shown that this herb enhances stamina and reduces cortisol produced as a result to post exertion exercises.

(References – "Medicinal Plants of the World"; Ben-Erik van Wyk & Michael Wink; 2009) – (Medical Herbalism; The Science and Practice of Herbal Medicine; David Hoffman; 2003)

(Adaptogens: Herbs for Strength, Stamina, and Stress Relief by Eric Hamilton Feb 12, 2013) – (University of Maryland Medical Center: Stress – Lifestyle Changes.

(MayoClinic.com; Stress – Constant Stress puts Your Health at Risk.)

<u>**Notes**</u>: *Try and keep workouts no more than 1 hour and train efficiently and intensely as you can, studies do show that cortisol levels rise and peak after 1 hour of intense training.*

Spike your insulin levels after your workouts by consuming high glycemic carbohydrates that will help lower post induced high cortisol levels after training. Since insulin interferes with cortisol and it may enhance cortisol removal from the blood stream.

One other thing that we have to be concerned with is over training during your workouts. We have to keep in mind that as we age our recuperative abilities are not what they were when you were young, so we have to be as diligent and efficient as we can be. That is another "key" component that we have to keep in mind as we're working out. So, with the information given to you about cortisol, we now have a good understanding of how cortisol can ruin our chances of gaining muscle quickly.

<u>Over training goes hand in hand with cortisol</u>. By keeping your workouts up to one hour and taking the proper supplements to help keeping cortisol under control, we can now minimize its effect on our capability to gain muscle rapidly. You'll thank me in the end

when its all said and done.

CHAPTER 12

Weight Training Principles For Bodybuilding

Without a constant change in your training regimen, the body will absolutely go stale. The likely reason? You haven't thrown anything new into the mix. Muscles need to be shocked, challenged or lets say waken up, because just like anything else, it will eventually get boring and then we wonder why we're not making any muscle gains. Progression is the key to new muscle growth, and we do have the blue-print for you here in this chapter.

The Weider principles is a list of weightlifting truisms gather and honed by the father of bodybuilding "Joe Weider" that have stood the test of time through the years past. There are 24 of these principles, and it is highly recommended that you look into these principles to learn and advance your muscle building efforts.

Muscle Priority Training – this is working out the most weakest or particular body part that needs more emphasis on building up.

Progressive Overload – in making additional muscle gains you need to work harder in a progressive manner from one workout to the next trying to increase the weight in each session, doing more reps, sets, or decrease your rest periods between sets.

Pyramid Training – is incorporating a range of lighter to heavier weights for each exercises. Starting out light with higher reps of (12-14) to warm-up the muscle, then gradually increase the weight in each successive set while lowering your reps (6 to 8). You can also reverse this procedure by moving-from high weight and low reps to low weight and high reps, aka reverse pyramiding.

Instinctive Training – is experimenting to developing an instinct as to what works best for you by using your training results along with past experiences to fine tune your program. Go by feeling in the gym, if you don't feel like doing biceps because you feel they may have not recovered enough from the last workout, then do another body part instead.

Flushing Training Technique – is training one body part with multiple exercises (3-4) before you train another. The "flushing" is your sending a maximum amount of blood and nutrients to that particular area of the muscle to stimulate growth.

Isolation Training – this technique allows you to work an individual muscle without involving adjacent muscles or muscle groups. A press down for triceps rather than close grip bench press is an example of an isolation movement.

Cycle Training – devoting portions of your training to specific goals for strength, mass or getting cut. This can help decrease your chance of injury and add a variety to your routine. Cycle periods of high intensity training and low intensity to allow for recovery and create new gains.

Elective Training – incorporating a diverse set of variables, such as sets, reps and exercise schemes into your workout. Body part should utilize both mass-building multi-joint moves and single joint exercise's.

Continuous Tension – this is done by not allowing a given muscle to rest at the top or bottom of the movement by controlling both the positive and negative portions of a rep and avoiding momentum to maintain constant tension throughout the entire range of motion.

Peak Contraction – squeeze your contracted muscle isometrically at the end point of a rep to intensify effort. Hold the weight in the fully contracted position for up to two seconds at the top of an exercise.

Super Set Principle – performing sets of two exercises for the same or different muscle groups back to back with no rest period in between.

Tri-Set Principle – is done by performing three consecutive exercises for a particular muscle non-stop without resting.

Giant Sets – this is done by performing four particular exercises for a one muscle group performed in back to back fashion without rest in between.

Burns – continuing a set past the point at which you can lift the weight through a full or partial range of motion with a series of rapid partial reps. Do this as long as your muscles can still move the weight, even if its only for a few inches.

Cheating Principle – using a momentum (a slight sling of the weight) to overcome a sticking point as you fatigue near the end of a set. While doing barbell curls, for example, you might be able to perform only eight strict reps to failure. A subtle swing of the weight or a slightly faster rep speed may help you get 1 to 2 additional reps. Cheating principle is normally used for advanced bodybuilders.

Forced Reps – have a training partner assist you with the reps near the end of a set to help you train past the point of momentary muscular failure as your training partner assists you in the lift of the movement. Example, when performing a maximum set of reps, say 6 to 8, he will then help with a slight lift getting past 6-8 reps, say to 10 reps with his help.

Negative Training Principle – resist the downward motion of a heavy weight. For example, on the bench press, use a weight that's 15% to 25% heavier than you can typically handle, and fight the resistance on the way down of the movement. Then have your training partner assist you on the positive portion of the rep helping you on the way up of the exercise.

Partial Reps – do reps involving only a partial range --- at the top, in the middle or at the bottom of the movement.

Pre-Exhaustion Principle – pre-exhaust a muscle with a single-joint exercise before performing a multi-joint movement. In leg training, you can start with leg extensions (which target the quads) before starting a set of squats (which also work the glutes and hamstrings).

Rest – Pause Principle – take brief rest periods during a set of a given exercise to squeeze more reps out of a set by using a weight that you can lift for 2-3 reps, rest as long as 20 seconds, then try another 2-3 reps. Take another brief rest and go again for as many reps you can handle, and repeat one more time.

Descending or Drop Sets – after completing your reps in a heavy set, quickly strip an equal amount of weight from each side of the bar or select lighter dumbbells. Continue to do reps until you fail, then strip more weight off to complete more reps.

Iso-Tension Principle – between sets (or even between workouts), flex and hold various muscles for 6-8 seconds, keeping them fully contracted before releasing. Competitive bodybuilders use this technique usually to enhance their posing ability through increased muscle control.

CHAPTER13

Best Exercise's For Muscle Mass

There are many exercises that will basically build muscle mass, but we are going to actually list those that many bodybuilders rely on for muscle mass. The best way to do that is by specific movements as mentioned in the begging of the first chapter. These specific exercises target the large muscle groups of the body. These exercise's for maximum muscle growth that are considered the best all around mass producers, that have been used by the best bodybuilders of all time. They have and will always be the number one exercises for the single purpose of how to gain weight fast, and nothing compares to that, and they will never be bested. Basic or compound exercises allow you to lift more weight, and the more weight you lift, the bigger you will become.

With that in mind, what are the compound exercises which are the ones that are the best for maximum muscle mass? Compound lifts, or multi-joint lifts, are weightlifting exercises that force you to use more muscle groups, preferably 3 or more. For example, the bench press is a compound exercise, although the primary muscle used is the chest muscles, your shoulder, triceps are also helping you lift the weight.
The tricep push downs, however, are an isolation movement or single-joint exercise that basically isolates the triceps, and triceps only, a single muscle. Since this exercise just isolates a single muscle, your triceps, it doesn't involve or stimulate nearly as much muscle growth as compound lifts would do.

Although they are many other different compound movements, you must focus on only those that stimulate the most amount of muscle and allow you to lift the heaviest weight possible. Here are the best compound exercises or mass building exercises that you must include in your training regimen if you expect to build maximum muscle mass in the shortest amount of time. This is the main focus of this book, building maximum muscle mass in the shortest amount of time. If you follow this program and apply what you've learned by reading this book, you will then not be disappointed, I assure you!

If your workouts do not include any of these compound movements, well then don't expect to grow. Ask any serious bodybuilder in the gym and they will tell you that compound exercises is a sure fire way to build muscle mass fast. One of the greatest advantage of compound exercises is you can do a whole body workout in just a few exercises in just a few minutes. And in contrast to isolation exercises which usually focuses on only a single muscle group, compound exercises allows you to limit your isolation exercise sets for instance because you've already worked your muscle groups to a certain extent.

There is over 100 years of evidence that these compound exercises actually work faster, because compound movements stress the largest amount of muscle groups the quickest.

"Key" Compound Exercises For Muscle Mass

Here are the grand daddy of all muscle mass compound exercises that you must include in your training regimen if you expect to build muscle mass in the least amount of time.

1) **Barbell bench press** – (targets -chest muscles, shoulders and triceps)
2) **Squats, Barbell** - (targets the whole leg muscles, quads, hamstrings, and calves)
3) **Barbell rowing** – (back muscles, lats-upper and lower rear delts, and biceps)

4) **Pull-ups** – (back muscles, biceps, rear deltoids)
5) **Military press** – (shoulders, front deltoids & medial deltoid, triceps, traps)
6) **Deadlifts** – (leg muscles, lower back, biceps, forearms)
7) **Parallel Bar Dips** – (complete chest muscles, triceps, and shoulders)
8) **Power Cleans** – (forearms, back, legs, traps, biceps, shoulders)
9) **Clean & Jerk** – (forearms, biceps, triceps, shoulders, traps, legs)

Try starting some of these of exercises by adding lets say, an example routine would be like this – a whole body workout. Beginning with a warm up of course, light cardio (treadmill 10 minutes). **Workouts will be 3 days a week – Monday-Wednesday-Friday's, Rest days are Tuesday, Thursday, Saturday and Sunday (rest days are most important)**

Sample Beginner's Weightlifting Routine

1) *Squats** – 2-3 sets of 10-12 reps
2) *Bench Press** – 2—3 sets of 6-8 reps
3) *Dips* – 2-3 sets of 8-10 reps
4) *Pull-ups** - (same as above)
5) *Barbell rowing* *- (same)
6) *Miltary press** - (same)
7) *Upright Rowing* -(same)
8) *Barbell curls* - (same)
9) *Close grip tricep press downs* - (same)

*Note: The Asterik * mark signifies the mass compound movements.*

As you can see in the sample routine above we have listed 5 of the compound exercises along with some isolation movements. Two to three months of this say, sample routine would be an ideal type of workout that literally targets muscles from head to toe. Emphasis should always be on a progressive light increase in weight, especially on the compound movement exercises. Try not to be sloppy but always perform your exercises as strictly as possible. The only weight lifting principle that will be employed here would be the progressive-overload principle. This is how your going to build your muscle mass as quickly as possible.

You can of course vary your sets and reps as you go along and get comfortable with what your trying to do. Most importantly try and not to exceed, to be in the gym for over an hour, 45 minutes to one hour maximum is allowed, anything after that will be counter productive and will only lead you to over training syndrome. Use the clock as your intensity booster keeping an eye out for your time allotted for your workouts.

Intensity and **progression** are **two key important factors** to consider along with the gate keeper, the clock!

This is what builds your muscles efficiently and gets you the results that you would want to see in no time, trust me and you will be very happy with the results. I have never met any one that's utilized this system and managed to gain any muscle mass, not in over 30 years of training.

Training For Maximum Size

When training for muscle size you have to remember that everyone is different and everyone responds differently to different training methods, however when it comes to maximum muscle size everyone will respond to a progressive over-load principle. Its just natural for muscles to grow when a heavy load is placed on them, muscle cells will split and grow new muscle cells to accommodate the load placed on it.
Give some of these mass techniques a try to kick start your muscles if you have reached a plateau.

1) <u>**Training for size:**</u> Reps are 4 to 8 range. Anything lower than that is good for strength, and when a weightlifter trains for 1-3 reps they are getting their tendons, ligaments and central nervous systems stronger, however you are not really causing any muscle hypertrophy in the 1 to 3 rep range. At best your laying the foundation for superior muscular growth. So what is the best solution to cause muscle hypertrophy? The 4-8 repetition range stimulates muscles instead of ligaments and tendons. Which means the 4 to 8 rep range is the best method to cause muscle cell growth.

2) <u>**Training for shape**</u> is a matter of keeping your repetition range between 10 to 12 and anything after that will increase your definition status.

3) <u>**How to Get Huge Leg Muscles**</u> – One of the best ways to cause your leg muscles to grow fast is by doing deep full heavy squats for reps of 20 being the maximum weight you can handle. Example – lets say that you can squat 300lbs for 15 reps, next time try to do 300lbs for 20 reps. This will cause amazing growth to your legs as as well as stimulating upper body growth too.

4) <u>**High Intensity Training -(HIT)**</u> Is doing an exercise to an all out single set to failure. This is also known as "High Intensity Training" (HIT) means to lift weights for only two days a week, and performing two exercises only. What you are doing is, trying to do two all out exercises for the most intense sets of your life. Such as, if your bench is a 405lbs max for 1 repetition, instead reduce the weight to down like 225 lbs and take 5 seconds to bring it down to your chest and

then go up slowly with it for a set of 12 reps to failure. By training this way and doing heavy negative overload principle for reps can also help you attain growth.

Always remember to rest and recover properly as this type of training can really tear down muscle tissue, take also lots of supplements to support your muscle growth, because the bottom line is, if you do not recuperate correctly then you will tear down muscle tissue and they will never get a chance to heal and growth.

Example of High Intensity Training (HIT)

Day One

1) Squats –315 x 20 reps, then you do a 1 rep max of 350lbs
2) Dead lifts –315 x 20, then you do a 1 rep max 405lbs.

Day Two

1) Bench Press – 255 x 8, 350lbs x 1 rep max.
2) Military Press – 185 x 6-8 reps, 225 1 rep max.
3) Bent Over Rowing – 225 x 6-8 reps, 275 x 1 rep max.

Note: Don't forget your post workout meal with a protein shake to follow.

4) **Stretching** - stretch after every muscle group is finished working out. This will help to improve muscle recovery that much quicker allowing for maximum blood flow to muscle cell tissue.

5) **Progressive Over-load** – The most important aspect of muscle growth is to overload the muscle with heavy weight more than what you are accustomed to, or decrease your rest periods in between sets.

6) **Do Power Lifting Exercise's** – for a short while, 4 weeks of this type of training will shock your muscles into new growth.

(Example)

1) Full Squats -
2) Bench Press -
3) Power Cleans-
4) Clean & Jerk -
5) Dead Lifts -
6) High Pulls -

This routine you can do *3 days a week*, working out the whole body. Your mind set should be heavy weights with *low reps of 4 to 6, and 1 rep max* at the end of each last set per exercise.

CHAPTER 14

Bodybuilding Tips; Training, Diet, Protein Shake Formula's, and Workout Supplements

This chapter will basically summarize some of the important facts to consider and help you to remember key points made throughout the previous chapters.

As a general bodybuilding rule, always make it a habit to do more compound exercises than isolation exercises. It is the compound exercises that build the majority of muscle tissue, and should always be performed first at the start of your workouts while your fresh and rested.

When training for muscle mass, always try and increase the work load by making the weight heavy as you can for the recommended repetitions of 4 to 6 reps.

Big Movements build big muscles, like bench press, squats, dead lifts, military press, rowing, pull ups, high pulls, and dips. Think of these as the exercise staple.

Building muscle, also involves stretching after every exercise performed. Stretching the muscle at the bottom of the movement and at squeezing the muscles it at the top.

Barbell Squats is a must, you have to perform this exercise, because squating is the biggest muscle building exercise there is. Its not so much for the legs, but also stimulates upper body growth as well. Squating involves so many muscles and is so taxing on the body that it forces the body to release growth hormone (GH).Which basically affects all muscle growth of the body, not just the legs. Was also considered "Arnold Schwarzenegger's" favorite exercise of all.

Always try and aim for improving certain aspects of your training workout from the previous week before. It can be extra reps, sets, more weight, etc.

Don't over train, more is not necessarily better, meaning more time spent in the gym. Go by how your body feels, you should be leaving the gym feeling as though you could do more. If you don't feel that way, but feel tired by the end of your workout. Then that is a sign that you've done too much! Re-evaluate your training program and see where your doing too much of certain body parts.

Keeping a train log of your workouts can become like your training partner, make sure you log the amount of weights used to keep better track of your progress. Make notes of certain points that you've noticed. Keep track of what is working for you and what isn't working.

Prioritize your training to bring up certain lagging body parts, make them your main focus on what needs improving.

Plan your workouts ahead, knowing what your going to do before you walk into the gym. Thinking about what you what to achieve.

Most important, be consistent in your scheduled workouts, try not to miss any workouts. Remember you only get out of it, what you put into it, so don't miss any workouts!

Learn your diet, when you start your muscle building diet plan, you need to learn Every thing about the food you are going to be eating. How many calories, carbs, proteins, and fats in every food group. The more you learn about your food, the easier it will be to plan your diet for muscle growth and fat loss.

Treat your meals like fuel for your body.

Keep well hydrated, make sure your drinking enough fluids (3 liters). ***Remember dehydration inhibits muscle growth, and can cause muscle wasting syndrome***.

By keeping the body well hydrated, you will ensure extra cellular fluid within the muscle cells. Make sure your getting a balanced intake of essential fatty acids, omega3's, omega 6, and omega 9. Look for a product called Udo' Choice, perfect supplement!

1) Take advantages of the anabolic phase of your training sessions by making it a habit of taking the proper nutrients an hour before training, during training, and especially after training;

2) *Pre-workout nutritional requirements* – (one hour before) include 3-5 grams of creating (kre-alkalyn version), *5 to 10 grams of branch amino acids, 5 to 10 grams of Glutamine, 25 to 30 grams of protein shake mixed in skim milk or water.*

3) During workout nutritional aid – *cyto-max carb drink with a nitric oxide booster (citrulline malate, beta-alanine).*

4) <u>Post-workout nutritional shake</u> – *30 to 40 grams of Hydrolyzed protein (15 minute absorption time), two table spoons of Flax Seed Oil, 5-10 grams of BCAA's, 5-10 grams of Glutamine, Bromelian or papaya enzymes mixed in skim milk 12 to 16 ounces, and 6 ounces of coconut milk.*

5) <u>Bedtime nutritional aid</u> – *100% casein protein powder (for positive nitrogen retention), 5 to 10 grams of glutamine for over night recovery, two table spoons of flax seed oil for protein metabolism and digestion, and glutathionine 500mgs for over night recovery process.*

In trying to gain muscle mass, make sure you eat every 2-3 hours.

Your carbohydrate intake should be of complex carbs, (except with your post-workout meal/shake) to provide you with long lasting energy levels.

Supplement your diet with a good multi-mineral, anti-oxidants, and glutathione for your immune system. Will help with the recovery process.

Use dextrose in your protein shakes, dextrose is the simplest of simple carbs and it can give you the best possible insulin spike, which nothing else compares.

If you are over 35, its not a bad idea to supplement your diet with a testosterone boosters. As this is the average age testosterone starts to wind down.

If you have a skinny build, it would be a good idea to use a weight gaining supplement. They do give you a huge boost in calories, along with the essential nutrients like vitamins, minerals, and ample amounts of protein, carbs, and essential fats. Good brand weight gainer's are <u>*"Optimum Nutrition's-Serious Mass Gainer", and "BSN's - True Mass"* both are equally as good, but I like the taste of "BSN's" products.</u>

Protein Shake Muscle Building Formula's

Protein is by far and away the most important nutrient you'll need to build muscle period. Muscle is protein and protein is muscle. Before steroids came into effect bodybuilders of many years ago relied on high quality protein foods to build muscle-mass. They used what nature provided for them in the form of eggs, meats, beans, fish, milk, and high fat dairy products. It was in the 1950's that protein powder was starting to make head way by a true nutritional genius, Rheo H. Blair (real name, Irvin Johnson), who invented protein powder and eventually amino acid tablets. Some of his recipes on protein shakes are still being used today by many bodybuilders.

Also some of the greatest bodybuilders of the 1950's, 60's, and 70's used his protein supplements and followed his nutritional program to achieve the best shape of their lives. Among his success stories are the legendary Larry Scott, Dave Draper, Frank Zane, Steve Davis, Don Howorth, Sergio Olivia, and many others. As an avid bodybuilder himself, Rheo Blair began researching weight training and nutrition, in which he found his true calling in life. He concentrated on the nutritional aspects of bodybuilding searching across the United States for nutritionists and began experimenting on himself and other bodybuilders.

His quest was combining the perfect foods for a muscle building formula for anabolic growth. He believed that "Mother's Milk" to be the perfect food for human growth, mix matching combinations of milk, whey and whole eggs in an effort to match the perfect amino acid ratio of human mother's milk. The food he came across to being the most closest to was not cow's milk, but the egg. Finally, his efforts and information finally paid off and his protein shakes, powders, and recipes became the most sought after in the bodybuilding world.

Then came the addition of soy protein formula's along with another weight lifting legend, Bob Hoffman who also sold and manufactured protein powder supplements in the mid 1950's. At that time also, it was considered a discovery in the science of protein. The Wander Company which produced and sold "Ovaltine" had created a milk and egg protein powder called "Optipro", which sold in drug stores throughout the US. Rheo Blair had always believed that milk and eggs were superior for muscle building. This was soon to be the start of the protein revolution that grew into a multi-million dollar industry.

Today we have all sorts of protein powders ranging from meat-based protein powders, milk, soy, egg, plant-based, and even vegetable based protein powders. And so the supplement world of bodybuilding nutrition evolved with high-tech protein powders never thought possible years ago. The next step in the evolution of protein powders will be interesting to see what they will come up with. However, till then you have available to you some of the most complex formula's to use for whatever circumstances for bodybuilding purposes. Below you will find some protein nutrient dense formula's that you can utilize to gain muscle growth quickly. Some of these are from Rheo Blair's protein recipes that he would teach his prized pupils back in the day, I think you will find most interesting.

Meal Replacement Protein-Shake (can be used breakfast time, lunch, dinner)

1 and a half cup of skim milk or whole milk
1 heaping tablespoon of Raw natural peanut butter
half a banana
1 tablespoon of Raw unfiltered honey
5-10 grams of BCAA's
5-10 grams Glutamine
2 scoops of Protein blend, whey/casein
Bromelian or papaya powder

Rheo H. Blair's Milk & Egg Protein Mix *-(consume 3x a day)*

- One cup of whole milk
- B-complex powder
- 2 tablespoons of Flax Seed Oil
- Milk & Egg protein powder (2 scoops)
- teaspoon vanilla extract

or

- 1 cup of milk
- 1 cup cream
- 3 scoops of Egg protein powder
- Peptain HCL

Protein Pudding Recipe

- Half cup of protein powder (milk & egg) can be eaten as an extra protein snack in between meals.
- 8 oz's of cream
- 2 oz milk
- 1 tablespoon vanilla extract
- Fruit of choice optional.
- Mix ingredients to a pudding like consistency and eaten with a spoon.
-

Growth promoting Protein Shake for Rapid Size!

1 cup protein powder whey hydrolysates 2 scoops for 45 grams of protein
5-10 grams of BCAA's
10 grams of Glutamine
5-10 grams of Colostrum (essentials growth promoting factors)
2 table spoons Flax seed oil
bromlian or papaya enzymes

(and watch your muscles grow!)

Note: *These examples are some of the idea's that you can incorporate to devise a high powered protein formula that will help enhance your growth potential. Always try and include some kind of essential fats with your protein powder shakes like – peanut butter, flax seed oil, coconut milk or oil, proteins need fats to be digested and absorbed efficiently.*

Also, **BCAA's** at least 5 to 10 grams 2x a day, especially on workout days. **Glutamine** also should be included, a very necessity item for new muscle growth and for recovery purposes.

Colostrum is another valuable aid because of its various growth factors for lean muscle growth and for its GH and IGF-1 release. Always use at least 5 grams per serving with your protein shakes. It will make a big difference in your muscle development.

By incorporating **BCAA's (Leucine especially), Glutamine, and Colostrum** into any protein shake mix along with some essential fats, enzymes, can really super charge your growth potential. You can even add nutrient dense products like **Bee Pollen granules** to fortify your shake even more potently. Bee Pollen has natural vitamins, minerals, and amino acids to make for a healthy serving of a highly charged protein shake.

Note: Rheo's protein formula's were based on the highest quality of protein available in terms of supporting "human growth" and well being that would be found in mother's milk "colostrum". His preferred liquid for mixing his protein was half and half, reason being, nature seems to indicate that protein and fat should be taken in even balance with an equal amount of fat. Milk itself, with 3% protein is balanced with an equal amount of fat, like wise eggs, meat, etc.

By mixing protein with half whole milk and half heavy cream we restore some of the fat removed during processing and we achieve a product more normally balanced as to proportions of protein and fat. Remember, you are not actually drinking half & half when you follow this suggestion, the protein with the half & half makes a "milk" drink which le milk in the balance of protein and fat. It is thick and creamy because it is concentrated. Rheo's concept on protein absorption was way a head of his time.

CHAPTER 15

Important & Necessary Bodybuilding Supplements

If your goal is to gain muscle mass and establish overall health, then your best bet is to consider choosing <u>whole foods first and supplements second</u>. Whole foods can create and provide almost the same health response as some supplements can. Their called supplements for a reason, and that's to supplement our daily diet with nutrients that we can not get from certain foods.

So based on what your trying to establish health wise, and muscle building, you should then plan on creating a sound diet that will compliment your body with the raw materials it needs to build muscle and a training program that will encourage muscle growth. <u>You build muscle through diet and training</u>. By just taking supplements alone devoid of food will only lead to poor health and all kinds of health problem. Bodybuilders in the past have always created incredible physiques without supplements back in their day. They only had whole quality foods at their disposal, which worked well for them on building muscle.

The best muscle enhancing supplements, used correctly, can also give the body much more muscle building power when combined with the right foods. Balance is the key!

Without the proper muscle building nutrition, your muscles simply will not grow. When it comes to building muscle, there are a few that will suit our purpose in enhancing muscle building capabilities. <u>I will list those according to what they do and how to use them to your advantage.</u>

<u>High Quality Protein powders</u> – Fast absorbing whey proteins like isolates, and hydrolysates for their extremely high bio-availability important for muscle growth. <u>To be used prior to workouts, during workouts and immediately after workouts</u>. Protein builds muscle tissue, and new muscular growth. It should be the first supplement bought when embarking on a weight lifting or bodybuilding program. (recommended brands of quality are listed in earlier chapters).

<u>Whey protein</u>, undisputed king of protein powders, which are fast acting, easily digested, high in branch chain amino acids, especially Leucine, and contains subcomponents of microfractions that provide benefits above and beyond. Whey isolates have no fat, lactose, and the whey peptides have been hydrolyzed for even faster digestion and absorption.

<u>Casein proteins</u> – slower acting, anti catabolic (rich in glutamine), best to take at am hours and at bedtime. Dorian Yates was a big advocate of using casein proteins as a more effective source of protein. He won 6 Mr. Olympia's using micellar casein as his protein source. The benefits of casein is greater muscle retention, fat loss and a higher quality of protein that protects muscle tissue breakdown which is a big, big, block lifted for getting massive.

Casein doesn't provide whey's anabolic response, but does provide a more steady stream of amino acids, but to maximize the best of both worlds, combine casein with whey protein and in doing so you will benefit from a high leucine content of whey and a high glutamine content that of casein giving you a steady feed of growth enhancing amino acids. Micellar casein hydrolysates are the premier choice in casein proteins.

<u>Egg Protein</u> – considered the gold standard also assimilates at the rate of whey protein which leads to a rapid increase in plasma amino acids, eggs also are an excellent source of vitamins and minerals, essential fats, and micro-nutrients.

<u>Important:</u> Your post-workout protein shake is the best time the body can absorb the most amounts of protein. The second best time is at bedtime while sleeping. The third best time is early morning hours upon rising.

<u>Creatine Monohydrate</u> – Without question a worthy supplement that does contribute to muscle gains and strength. A natural ***myostatin inhibitor/blocker*** is the reason that we're able to gain several of pounds of muscle relatively fast when you first take creatine. Research is showing creating isn't just a "pump and go" supplement that stores energy. But that creating is a real anabolic, responsible for real increases in muscle protein production inducing more IGF-1 in muscle tissue.

Look for the higher quality versions that are micronized, and the absorbed enhancing with insulin potentiators, kre-alkalyn versions, are all great supplements.

Sometimes experimenting with the correct version that agrees with your own specific bio-chemstry works best. No need to load up as always advertised, just a market publicity campaign to increase sales. 5 grams of creating daily would be an acceptable dosing regimen and after two weeks can be taken once daily to ensure adequate muscle stores of creating.

<u>Glutamine</u> – Another proven supplement without question as well that serves muscle development very well when used correctly. Is the most abundant amino acid in our intracellular fluid (ICF), composing more than 60% of any other amino acid in muscle tissue. 70 to 80% of the immune tissues in the body are located in the stomach (gastrointestinal tract). Its benefits and metabolic properties are extraordinary, benefiting the gastro-intestinal tract, stomach lining, liver, immune system ***(precursor to glutathionine)***, nitrogen retention, oxidative stress, muscle preservation, injuries, anti-metabolic, and much more!

More of glutamine intake is needed if muscle growth and size is to be achieved, very important if looking to get to the next level of muscular development and should always be included in any training. Practical applications for glutamine supplementation are: pre-work out, post workout, pre-sleep, post sleep, and any time you are sick increase your glutamine levels. Overt raining is also a sign that your glutamine levels are falling short.

(references- Antonio J, street C. Glutamine: a potentially usefull supplement for athletes. Can J Appl Physiology. 1999 Feb. 24(1): 1-14.)

Glutathionine (GSH)– A very potent antioxidant that helps to protect muscle tissue from free radical damage. A must supplement to use to help recovery from intense workout sessions. Speeds up healing of damaged muscle tissue broken down from training. Is also the body's master anti-oxidant protecting bodily functions to maintain a healthy lifestyle. Will definitely make a difference in your muscular growth and health. Take daily, 500mg to 1,000mgs.

Note: With the addition of a high quality protein supplement powder, will help you raise your glutathione levels up.

Enzymes – Because of the poor food choices people often make that are devoid of naturally occurring enzymes typically found in foods. Most people, young and old are deficient in the life enhancing catalyst's that help our body utilize the vitamins, minerals, essential fats, and nutrients we get from foods.

Bloating after high fat and protein rich meals are a sure sign of deficiency in enzymes. If taking your protein shakes often results in bloating, it is a sign that you may lack vital enzymes and/or stomach acids that are needed to digest the proteins, fats, and carbs. Supplementing with pancreatic enzymes or a multi-enzyme formula will help ensure proper absorption of the vital amino acids so necessary for health and muscle growth. Remember, we are what we absorb from the foods we eat. Enzymes are a very important necessity. Ensure that you eat enzyme rich foods like fruits, vegetables, yogurts, or supplement your diet with enzyme supplements.

Branch Chain Amino Acids (BCAA's) – (*leucine, isoleucine, and valine*)
Important for immediate muscle recovery used to build new proteins after hard training as a primary muscle building insurance policy. BCAA's should always be part of anyone's supplement list for noticeable muscle density. Add 5 to 10 grams with your protein powder shake, pre-workout, post-workout, or during training.(recommended brands – Optimal Nutrition, Twin Labs, Country Life, AllMax Nutrition.

L-Leucine – One of the 3 branch chain amino acids that is unique in its ability to stimulate skeletal muscle protein synthesis having a 10 fold greater impact on protein synthesis than any other amino acid. Leucine activates a major complex in the anabolic pathway called mammalian target rapamycin (mTOR), as the main amino acid sensor of the cell. Adding leucine to a protein rich meal or shake can further increase the rate of skeletal muscle protein sythsis. Athletes 30 years and older will benefit from leucine use in the dose of 10 grams or greater. (See earlier chapters on leucine use for further information).

Omega 3 Fish Oil - Omega 3 fatty acid will help improve performance and build new muscle by helping support healthy blood circulation to allow nutrients such as proteins, and carbohydrates reach muscle tissue and help also to promote healthy cardiovascular care. Fish oil, will also help to minimize excess estrogen build up from testosterone increases. Eating a variety of fish like salmon, halibut, tuna, mackerel, cod, and sardines will help support your Omega 3 content in your muscle building efforts.(recommended brands – calrson's omega 3's, solgar, source naturals. Take with your daily meals.

Vitamin Mineral Supplement – A good vitamin and mineral supplement will help ensure you getting the proper amounts of vitamins and minerals from your daily diet, especially when training with a high intensity training program. It's basically a good insurance policy towards great health. Athletes in general have special dietary needs due to the heavy demands place on the body from the physical resistance work.(good brands are – Twin Labs, Country Life, All One, Source Naturals, Solgar. Take with food.

Nitric Oxide Boosters That Work - Nitric oxide, a radical gas produced in the body that functions as a key biological messenger that plays an incredible role in the growth of muscle tissue that contains several benefits for our body's over all growth and development. A bodybuilding workout program would not be complete if nitric oxide supplements were not mentioned and/or used.

By supplementing your workouts with nitric oxide boosters you will help to ensure your muscle to recuperate much faster after workouts, which in turn leads to faster muscle growth. Nitric oxide supplements also help to enhance your muscle's pump and promote the fastest recovery of it.

I will list some of the proven nitric oxide supplements that actually work. And you might find in various nitric oxide formula's.

Beta-Alanine *** – The benefits of beta-alanine have been supported by scientific studies to increase muscular strength & power output, increase muscle mass, boost muscular anerobic endurance, and delay muscular fatigue. Most of the recent research is showing that 4 to 5 grams a day with an optimal loading phase of 6 grams per day for the first two weeks seems to be the correct amount of beta-alanine needed. It is also normal to feel the effects of beta-alanine from the first dose taken. After the first two weeks of loading a normal dose of 3 to 4 grams seems to be the correct maintenance dose.(Good brands are IntraXCell by Athletic

Edge Nutrition)

Citrulline Malate – Is another great supplement that often appears in many of the nitric oxide booster formula's on the sports supplement market because it works! Citrulline malate boosts nitric oxide much better than arginine and has been shown to lower blood pressure, boost stamina, reduce muscle soreness by 42%, increase cellular energy levels, and has the ability to increase muscular growth by making Leucine and other branch chain amino acids more effective, by sparing muscle tissue and by encouraging muscle growth.

Most of the studies performed showed that 3 to 5 grams to be an effective dose. Citrulline malate is also increasing in popularity and is catching on by many bodybuilding enthusiats.

Agmatine – Is a by product of L-Arginine that holds much more promise than its counterpart – L-Arginine does. It takes part in more metabolic processes than arginine with even much more benefits being discovered on a daily basis. The health and muscle building benefits to the athlete are enormous ranging from – a pain fighter, meaning it has analgesic effects during recuperation from injury, aids post workout recovery periods, increases insulin production, acts as an LH and GH enhancing agent, has anti oxidant properties, and modulates as a nitric oxide booster, removes ammonia waste by products from heavy amino acid use, and can aid in diabetes and obesity problems.

Agmatine is a serious product to be taken along your supplement program that can be of enormous help towards rapid muscular growth. Touted as the "Holy Grail" of supplements.

Now son,
Show me who stole your bike

Remember the key concepts pertaining to your metabolic geno-type body and learn to apply them the best to your advantage. Always keep the progressive overload principle in mind when training, that is the "Key" concept of making steady gains. Good luck to you, and here's wishing you a happy journey to muscular growth!

Good Luck To You!

Tony Xhudo, M.S./H.N./B.C.

Conclusion: This is your basic supplement list that will help you gain the muscle you so desire. Stick with it and be diligent in your effort and dedicate yourself to your goal at hand, results will be forth coming and to your liking. There are many supplements out there that for bodybuilding purposes, the selection is vast and never try to over burden yourself with some of the excess supplements that attach scientific jargon that will confuse you.

Once you learn the basic supplements for bodybuilding, then you can add and proceed within your budget to take your bodybuilding efforts to the next level. You basically have everything that you need in this book according to your body type to build a body that will be the envy of others.

Remember the key concepts pertaining to your metabolic geno-type body and learn to apply them the best to your advantage. Always keep the progressive overload principle in mind when training, that is the "Key" concept of making steady gains. Good luck to you, and here's wishing you a happy journey to muscular growth!

REFERENCES & RESOURCES

Ergo-log.com

*Am J Physiology
2006 Aug; 291(2): E381-*

*Endocrinol metab.
7*

*Strength Athletes Train
J Strength Cond res.
22*

*Better with Citrulline;
2010 may; 24(5): 1215-*

Top 10 foods in protein; USDA National Nutrient Data Base for Standard References, Release 20.

Whey protein; resources library – Milk Composition & Synthesis. (n.d.) Animal Sciences Classes. Retrieved march 29, 2013.

Dietary Protein, endurance exercise, and human skeletal-muscle protein turn over. Rodriguez NR, Visiocky LM, Gaine PC. Curr Opin Clin Nutr metab Care. 2007 Jan;10(1):40-5

Timmerman KL, Volpi E. Amino acid metabolism and regulatory effects in aging. Curr Opin Metab care. 2008 Jan;11(10;45-9.

Ergogenic Aids for Bodybuilding; Tony Xhudo, July21, 2012.

Nutritional Ergogenic Aids; Judy A. Driskell, Feb 13, 2009

The Anabolic primer; Ergogenic Enhancement for hardcore Bodybuilders. Gerad Thorne, Oct. 16, 2009.

Agmatine suppresses nitric oxide production in microglia. Abe K, Abe Y, and Saito H.

Amino Acids: Agmatine Sulfate. Zarandi M, Serfozo P, Zsigo, Bokser L, Janaky T, Olsen DB, bajusz S, & Schally Av. (1992). poten agnosists of growth hormone releasing hormone. Part 1. International Journal of peptide and protein research. 39(3), 211-7.

Progressive over load training, the concept of you; Chris Goulet, April 16, 2004; Bodybuilding.com

Progressive Overload: The Key To Muscle Growth; Sean Nalewanyj, December 10, 2012

<u>**Recommended Reading**</u>

Bigger Leaner Stronger: The Simple Science of Building the Ultimate Male Body by Michael Matthews

The Anabolic Primer: Ergogenic Enhancement For Hardcore Bodybuilders, Gerad Thorne, Oct. 16, 2009.

The New Encyclopedia of Modern Bodybuilding: The Bible of Bodybuilding, Arnold Schwarzenegger and Bill Dobbins.

Frank Zane Body Training Manual by Frank Zane

Iron Mind: Stronger Minds, Stronger Bodies by Randall J. Strossen

Anabolics: William Liewellyn

The Beginner's Guide to Bodybuilding: Cameron Hall

Muscle Bound: The Secrets to Natural Bodybuilding by Jason Zahn

CPSIA information can be obtained at www.ICGtesting.com
Printed in the USA
BVIW12n1317010217
475080BV00011B/60